23510

EMPOWERING EMPLOYEES THROUGH DELEGATION

The *Briefcase Books* Series

Managing Stress: Keeping Calm Under Fire
Barbara J. Braham

Business Negotiating Basics
Peter Economy

Straight Answers to People Problems
Fred E. Jandt

Empowering Employees through Delegation
Robert B. Nelson

The Presentation Primer: Getting Your Point Across
Robert B. Nelson
Jennifer Wallick

Listen for Success: A Guide to Effective Listening
Arthur Robertson

EMPOWERING EMPLOYEES THROUGH DELEGATION

Robert B. Nelson

IRWIN
Professional Publishing
Burr Ridge, Illinois
New York, New York

Senior sponsoring editor: Cynthia A. Zigmund
Project editor: Karen J. Nelson
Production manager: Jon Christopher
Designer: Mercedes Santos
Art manager: Kim Meriwether
Typeface: 11/13 Palatino
Compositor: Wm. C. Brown Communications, Inc.
Printer: Arcata Graphics/Kingsport

Library of Congress Cataloging-in-Publication Data

Nelson, Robert B.
    Empowering employees through delegation.
       p.   cm.—(The Briefcase books series)
    Includes bibliographical references and index.
    ISBN 1-55623-847-9 (hardcover).—ISBN 0-7863-0199-6 (paperback)
    1. Delegation of authority. 2. Management I. Title.
    II. Series
    HD50.N463 1994
    658.4'02—dc20   93—5929

Printed in the United States of America

1 2 3 4 5 6 7 8 9 0 AGK 0 9 8 7 6 5 4 3

Briefcase Books Series

Research shows that people who buy business books (1) want books that can be read quickly, perhaps on a plane trip, commuting on a train, or overnight, and (2) feel their time and money were well spent if they get two or three useful insights or techniques for improving their professional skills or helping them with a current problem at work.

Briefcase Books were designed to meet these two criteria. They focus on necessary skills and problem areas, and include real-world examples from practicing managers and professionals. Inside these books you'll find useful, practical information and techniques in a straightforward, concise, and easy-to-read format.

This book and others like it in the Briefcase Books series can quickly give you insights and answers regarding your current needs and problems. And they are useful references for future situations and problems.

If you find this book or any other in this series to be of value, please share it with your coworkers. With tens of thousands of new books published each year, any book that can simplify the growing complexities in managing others needs to be circulated as widely as possible.

Robert B. Nelson

Series Editor

To Jennifer for her love, patience, and support

FOREWORD

by Ken Blanchard

My mission in life has been to be a conveyor of simple truths. It is for that reason that I'm please to be able to introduce the Briefcase Books series, which seeks to provide simple, practical, and direct answers to the most common problems managers face on a daily basis.

It has been my experience that in the field of business common sense is not common practice. So it is refreshing to find a series of books that glorifies common sense in dealing with people in the workplace.

Take the skill of listening. We all know that it is important to listen, yet how many of us actually do it well? I suggest it would be rare to find one in a hundred managers that is truly a good listener. Most people focus on what they are going to say next when someone else is talking. They would seldom if ever think to check what they thought they heard to make sure it is accurate. And they seldom acknowledge or attempt to deal with emotions when they occur in speaking with someone at work. These are basic errors in the use of this basic skill. And regardless of how much education or experience you have, you should know how to listen.

But how much training have you had on the topic of listening? Have you ever had a course on the topic? Have you ever tested your ability to listen? Have you ever discussed with others how you could listen better with greater comprehension and respect? Probably not. Even though this fundamental interpersonal skill could cripple the most talented individual if he or she is not good at it.

Fortunately, listening is just one of the fundamental skills singled out for its own volume in the Briefcase Books series. Others include books on making presentations, negotiating, problem solving, and handling stress. And other volumes are planned even as I write this.

The Briefcase Books series focuses on those basic skills that managers must master to excel at work. Whether you are new to managing or are a seasoned manager, you'll find these books of value in obtaining useful insights and fundamental knowledge you can use for your entire career.

Ken Blanchard

Co-author

The One Minute Manager

"If you ride a horse, sit close and tight.
If you ride a man, sit easy and light."

—*Poor Richard's Almanac*

Preface

HOW THIS BOOK WILL HELP YOU

Marjorie Blanchard, author of *Working Well*, tells the story of a manager who constantly brought home work. One evening his young daughter asked, "Mom, how come Daddy always brings home work?" Her mother replied, "Well, honey, he doesn't get it all done during the daytime." After a moment's thought, the girl asked, "Couldn't they put him a slower group?"

From time to time most of us face an oppressive workload and could stand to be placed in a "slower group." If this is a way of life for you, however, it may be a symptom of a more fundamental problem: POOR DELEGATION.

Are you constantly putting in long hours at work or on weekends? Has your social and family life dwindled to an occasional night out at McDonald's? Do your employees seem bored or perform poorly? If so, you may be lacking in delegation skills. And your work life will be out of control until you acquire them.

Inability to delegate undermines your effectiveness as a manager. It may cost you a promotion—or even your job!

Delegation is the best productivity skill a manager can master. Effective delegation reduces a manager's workload while developing employees' skills, knowledge, job satisfaction, and organizational commitment. The ability to delegate prepares employees who work for you to handle your responsibilities and simultaneously enables you to advance to other career opportunities within the organization. Delegating is a win-win activity. It produces more satisfied managers who are able to take on larger jobs at higher salaries *and* it produces more satisfied employees who are able to develop a broader range of skills and thus be prepared for promotion when you are.

In today's organizations, delegation is essential to empowering employees. As PepsiCo's Wayne D. Calloway says: "There are no silver bullets. But empowerment is important. You need that to feel, 'This is my business and my company, and I am the steward of these assets.' "[1] Adds Michael Dell, CEO and president of Dell Computer Corporation: "The winners in the next few decades will be the companies with the most empowered work forces."[2]

Fortunately, delegation skills are learnable. Putting delegation skills into practice may be difficult, but if you don't first learn what you're doing wrong, you'll never be able to improve. That's why you have this book.

This book explores the many facets of delegation: when to delegate, what to delegate, who to delegate to, how to delegate, and so on. As a practical handbook, it provides a step-by-step guide through the delegation process. It takes you through the essential steps of delegation and explains how to avoid crucial mistakes. It presents numerous examples from managers in business and provides checkpoints along the way so you can evaluate your progress.

This book is an invaluable reference for first-time supervisors or managers. It is also an essential tool for more experienced managers who feel overloaded or who think they're not getting the best effort out of their employees. Whether you are a new or experienced manager, the skills you learn from this book can help your career, your family . . . and your mental health.

Robert B. Nelson
San Diego, CA

Acknowledgments

Many thanks to Jennifer Wallick for her extensive help in developing this manuscript; Peter Economy, Sam Steinhardt, and Ted Schwartzman for reviewing drafts of this manuscript and making detailed suggestions for improvement; Bill Taylor, James Robinson, Ken Hughes, and Craig Garber for allowing themselves to be delegated the task of reviewing an earlier draft of this book; and Charlene Ables and Didem Ozonur for their research assistance.

Contents

What Delegation Can Do for You

Jim looked at the report, half in disgust and half in anger. "This isn't what I wanted," he thought to himself. "It's not what I asked for either." He dreaded having to spend another long weekend trying to salvage the report in time for Monday morning's meeting. "Why can't anyone ever do what I ask them to do?"

Jim and thousands of other managers like him face such situations every day. An employee's work must be redone, and the manager who must redo or reassign the work will hesitate to assign a similar task to the same individual again. Trust is lowered, time is wasted, and the real problem of ineffective delegation is allowed to continue. In the short run, it may seem that the employee is at fault, but in the long run it is the manager who failed.

If Jim had delegated the task more effectively, he would have had the results he expected when he expected them, and he would not be working over the weekend to redo the report. Both individuals would be less frustrated with their jobs. With better understanding and practice of delegation skills, managers and team members alike are more apt to succeed.

THE KEY TO SUCCEEDING AS A MANAGER

As a manager, you always have more responsibilities than time to carry them out. You can't adequately plan and perform every task you're responsible for. You must guard against wasting time on any nonmanagerial activity. The real measure of your effectiveness lies in your ability to get things done through other people—especially when you're not present.

Managers who don't delegate enough tasks find that they don't have enough time to complete their work. Managers who don't delegate *properly* find that they're dissatisfied with the tasks performed by their employees. And their employees lack enthusiasm and initiative when completing tasks delegated to them.

Consider the following story of a manager, Everett T. Suters, as reported in *Inc.* magazine:

> By the end of my second year in business, I was ready to give up. Although the company was growing, I felt tired and discouraged most of the time. We were always behind on our commitments to customers, and I used being too busy as an excuse for not planning. I mostly followed the squeaking-wheel principle, responding to the greatest pressure at the time. My appointment calendar was so tight that I was getting further behind with every emergency, and emergencies were happening with greater frequency.
>
> I was so overbooked that I couldn't meet with members of my staff on short notice or have any quality time with them. Whatever big ideas I had about participatory management went out the window. I had so many things on my mind, I found I wasn't even listening well when I did meet with my people. As for keeping them up to date on what was going on, it just didn't happen. At the same time, though, I began to feel some resentment and couldn't understand why the 30 or so people who worked for me didn't have the same

interest and drive I had. I was noticeably busier and was putting in longer hours than anybody else.

The fact is not only had I imposed unrealistic deadlines on the whole company, I was holding things up because I had assumed too many responsibilities. Instead of delegating to my staff, I was telling them what to do and later second-guessing and interfering with their work. That led to a constant parade of people in and out of my office, asking questions and checking things out with me, which meant I had even less time. Turnover was high, morale was low, especially among my best people.

Overachieving was taking a toll on my personal life as well. My moods were up, down, sideways. Every time I missed going home for dinner, I felt guilty. It seemed that my children were growing up, and I hadn't spent nearly enough time with them. And that is how, quite by accident, I came by my cure.

Until then, I had not taken a real vacation, but instead took a day or two at a time. By the end of that second year, I was so burned out I decided to take my family on a trip West for about a month. I assumed that when I returned my business would be in shambles, but that somehow I could put the pieces back together. To my amazement, things were running smoothly when I got back. It came to me as a revelation that if things could go this well without me in the office, they could continue to do so with me around.[1]

Mr. Suters is not alone. Too many managers waste time and money doing tasks that a team member could easily perform. In doing so, they limit their own effectiveness and fail to properly develop their employees. Mr. Suters was putting in long hours while the 30 or so people who worked for him were unmotivated, uncommitted, and not being used to their full potential. Such management inefficiency results in enormous costs to the organization.

Delegation is the most effective way to assign and co-ordinate the work done by many people. Delegation achieves greater results with less of your direct involvement. Delegation promotes cost effectiveness, job enrichment, higher morale, lower turnover, and more initiative from team members. Through effective delegation, you can devote yourself to what only you can do—manage.

THE REASON MOST MANAGERS FAIL

Mr. Suters realized when he returned from vacation that his inability to delegate effectively was taking its toll on both his organization's effectiveness and his personal life. He was spending time doing tasks that his staff could have been doing, leaving him with very little time or energy to do what he was supposed to be doing—managing his staff.

According to several surveys done on managerial success factors, the main reason managers fail is their inability to master the art of delegation. The ability to delegate is more important than any other skill you bring to your job. Effective delegation is more important than knowledge of organizational objectives, personnel administration, market distribution, company products and processes, corporate organization, or accounting principles.

Don G. Mitchell, former president of GTE and former chairman of General Time and Sylvania Electric Products, describes the two basic reasons that delegation fails. Either the person to whom you are delegating resists taking on responsibility or a manager secretly wants to keep the responsibility to himself. Too often, it's the latter.[2]

Failure to delegate is most noticeable with new managers. New managers are still trying to understand the position, feel insecure about their abilities, or both. When the inability to delegate is not corrected, team members adjust to their manager's ineffective style. They don't do assigned tasks as well as possible because they know their manager will redo it anyway, so the performance of both the manager and the group suffers. Managers who fail to learn delegation skills may kill their chances for promotion and risk their whole career.

GETTING WORK DONE THROUGH OTHERS

Effective delegation allows you—and your managers—to achieve your goals through others. But effective delegation is one of the most difficult challenges you will face. It's far more than issuing orders and walking away. Effective delegation requires careful planning, effective communication of responsibilities and expectations between you and your team members, and your commitment and participation to monitor and evaluate the delegation. Effective delegation is achieved through four basic steps: (1) preparing to delegate, (2) delegating tasks to team members, (3) monitoring the delegated work, and (4) evaluating the delegation.

Preparing to Delegate

To ensure success, you must spend time preparing to delegate. When preparing to delegate, you must develop the right attitudes about delegation, decide what to delegate, and decide who to delegate to.

For delegation to be effective, you must develop the right attitudes about delegation. Most important, you must be willing to take the risk of letting someone else be responsible for a job. This includes trusting team members to get the job done and being patient with team members who are learning new skills.

Another important step in preparing to delegate is deciding what tasks and responsibilities should be delegated. Delegate as many tasks as possible—to the lowest level possible. Allocate your time to managerial responsibilities only. All other responsibilities, if feasible, should be delegated to team members.

After deciding what tasks should be delegated, you need to decide who to delegate to. This includes deciding who has, or can obtain, all the necessary information to do the job. When deciding who to delegate to, take into account a team member's demonstrated skill, interest, and workload.

Delegating Tasks to Team Members

After you carefully prepare for the delegation, delegate the task by reaching a mutual agreement with the team member on the responsibilities being delegated and the standards of performance the team member will work by. Don't just tell or ask a team member to perform the task. Present the task in the way that is most certain of achieving the desired results. During this step, you and the team member must establish and agree on: (1) specific goals of the task, (2) performance standards of the task, (3) the level of authority granted for the completion of the task, (4) the obligation and commitment of the team member to complete the task, and (5) a reward system that recognizes good performance and holds the team member accountable for poor performance.

Monitoring the Delegated Work

Monitor every delegated task to communicate to the team member how well he is meeting performance standards and to identify and head off problems that he might not be able to handle. The amount and type of monitoring will vary from team member to team member and task to task. Mechanisms for monitoring delegation include regular status reports, regular staff meetings, and personal follow-up by the manager.

Evaluating the Delegation

As a follow-up to the delegation, appraise the completed task and discuss the evaluation with the team member. This is an opportunity for the team member to get feedback on his performance and for you to get feedback on your delegation skills.

BENEFITS OF DELEGATION

Although delegating is one of the most difficult aspects of any management job, there are many important benefits derived by the organization as well as the manager when tasks and responsibilities are properly delegated. Through delegation, you can ease the job of managing and thereby increase your own effectiveness and that of the work group. Following are specific benefits that the manager, team member, and organization derive from delegation skills.

Benefits for the Manager

Everybody wins with effective delegation, but delegation is especially important if you want to survive and grow in an organization.

Allows the manager to achieve more. Probably one of the most significant benefits is that you can achieve greater productivity. Through the proper selection, assignment, and coordination of tasks, you can mobilize resources to achieve more than would have been individually possible.

Allows time for managerial activities. Delegation gives you an opportunity to handle aspects of the job that no one else can do. These activities might include project planning, monitoring team members, and handling personnel problems as they arise. Using delegation, you can focus on doing a few tasks well rather than too many tasks poorly.

Increases managerial promotion potential. A final reason for learning delegation skills is for personal advancement. If you don't have people in the department who are trained to handle responsibilities, you will be shackled to one area and won't be considered for promotion.

John Henry Patterson, founder of National Cash Register Company, used to walk into his departments and order the managers to take two-week vacations. His motive: to determine whether a team member had been adequately trained to take over the supervisor's job on short notice. The key to such training, Patterson believed, was delegating—providing the team member with the experience, knowledge, and responsibility needed for a smooth transition.[3]

Managers who don't delegate don't have trained team members to take their places. Managers who aren't able to delegate at their current level won't be able to delegate at the next. Their ineffectiveness thus multiplies with each level in the organization.

Benefits for Team Members

Your team members are more highly motivated with effective delegation.

Develops team members' skills. Failure to effectively delegate deprives team members of opportunities to improve their skills and assume greater responsibility. Team members realize that they are not learning and gaining the experience they could. As a result, they may leave the firm for more challenging and supportive environments. Unfortunately, the most talented team members are the most likely to leave and those you least want to lose. A routine task for you is often a growth opportunity for a team member. Delegating a wide variety of assignments not only serves to train team members, it allows for backup personnel in times of emergency or termination of other employees. When others are well-versed in handling the responsibilities of different areas, you attain maximum flexibility and ensure that the project will not be at a standstill in your absence.

Increases team member involvement. Proper delegation encourages team members to understand and influence the work the department does. It allows team members a chance to incorporate their values in the workplace and, in many cases, to work on activities that especially interest them. Increasing team members' involvement in the workplace increases their enthusiasm and initiative.

Increases promotion potential. As with managers, a team member who receives extensive delegation will be ready and able to advance to new positions. In this regard, delegation serves both to train and to test an employee.

Benefits to the Organization

If both managers and team members benefit from delegation, it follows that the organization as a whole benefits.

Maximizes efficient output. When you delegate tasks according to the skills and abilities of each member of the work group, the department as a whole is likely to produce a higher level of work. Work will also be completed more efficiently. Delegation helps you make the best use of available human resources and achieve the highest possible rate of productivity. In addition, it allows new ideas, viewpoints, and suggestions to flourish.

Produces faster, more effective decisions. Effective delegation makes for faster, more effective decision making. An organization is most responsive to change in the environment when decisions are made by those individuals closest to the problems; that is, responsibility and decision making are pushed further down in an organization. Individuals closest to the problem have the most information on which to base an intelligent decision. Decision making can be achieved more expediently through delegation, thus allowing the organization to be more responsive and hence more competitive.

When team members participate in decision making, there is an increase in employee motivation, morale, and job performance. The greater the employee participation, the greater the employee commitment to the job and the organization!

Increases flexibility of operations. Effective delegation trains many people to do the same assignments. This overlap allows for greater flexibility of work assignments. When someone is absent or a crisis requires people to assist with tasks not regularly a part of their jobs, they will already be familiar with the assignment. Delegation prepares more individuals for promotion or rotation of responsibilities. And it allows you to appoint someone to supervise the work group when you're absent.

A FEW DEFINITIONS

Due to its intangible nature, delegation can be an abstract and confusing topic. So it's important to define terms.

Delegation

Delegation is defined as entrusting power and authority to a person acting as one's representative. During the process of delegating, team members are assigned a task or *responsibility*. They are given *authority* to complete the task, and they assume *accountability* for the completion of the task.

Responsibility

Dr. Lawrence L. Steinmetz, in his book, *The Art and Skill of Delegation*, states "responsibility consists of the obligation to undertake a specific duty or task within the organization." When defining responsibility with respect to delegation, it is important to distinguish between *ultimate responsibility* and *immediate responsibility*. You have the ultimate responsibility, or obligation, to see that work is properly completed and goals are met in a specific area of the company. A team member has the immediate responsibility for completing the delegated task. A team member who fails to complete the task is responsible for not doing so. You, however, bear ultimate responsibility. You need enough skill in delegation to be sure that all necessary work is completed as scheduled and needed for the effective operation of the department. For delegation to be effective, a team member must assume, and agree to be responsible for, completion of the assignment.

Authority

Authority in the context of delegation refers to the influence one derives from a title, rank, or privilege that gives a person the right to act or to tell another person to do something. Authority is a binding force in organizations. It is the foundation for giving and fulfilling responsibility. In practice, authority is defined as whatever influence people possess to enable them to get something done. This includes the official authority that comes from holding a specific position. Yet it can also include the authority someone derives from being the most experienced or knowledgeable about a certain task or topic. Still another meaning involves the personal authority derived from someone's personality and ability to work well with others. With any delegated task, it is usually necessary to be given an adequate, or commensurate, amount of authority to successfully complete the task. Authority also includes the ability to use whatever resources (people, equipment, money, and so on) necessary to complete an assignment. As John Nevin, former CEO of Firestone Tire & Rubber says: "If you want to drive a person crazy, the easiest way to do it is to give him a deep sense of responsibility and no authority. And the definition of terror is to give someone authority and no responsibility."[4]

Accountability

Accountability involves assessing a team member's performance on a delegated task. A team member effectively delegated a task must be held accountable if the task isn't completed accurately or on schedule. Accountability is essential for effective delegation. If team members aren't held accountable, the management function completely breaks down, and control and discipline within the organization are lost. According to Steinmetz:

> Many supervisors, managers, and executives fail to make effective delegations because they drop the ball at the point of accountability. They do not realize that accountability is the feedback loop which tells whether the delegated work has (or has not) been done. Obviously, remedial or corrective steps cannot be taken by the manager if he or she does not

know that some work has gotten behind, has not been finished, or has been performed at an unacceptable level. One of the principal reasons so many managers fail at making good work assignments and delegating effectively to their team members is that they do not use any feedback loop to tell them about the progress of the jobs or projects they have assigned.[5]

Managers sometimes don't enforce accountability because it is not a pleasant or easy thing to do. It involves monitoring tasks and confronting employees with possible reprimands on assignments that are poorly executed. It is much easier to focus on the future and on ways the task can be satisfactorily completed next time—or to ignore the situation completely.

Team Member

Throughout this book, the individual who reports to a manager or supervisor is referred to as a team member (or employee). This acknowledges the fact that, in most reporting relationships today, there is a mutual goal involved in the completion of any work assignment. Employees must be treated as equals in order for them to be productive and motivated. The best managers manage "with" and not "to" others.

EVALUATING YOUR DELEGATION STYLE

The following delegation checklist will help you evaluate your delegation skills and weaknesses. Check those comments that apply to you and your situation.

A Delegation Checklist

1. DEVELOP THE RIGHT ATTITUDE

   a. Maintain enough personal security in
   your own position so you don't feel
   threatened by delegation   _____

   b. Be willing to take risks   _____

   c. Trust your team members   _____

   d. Become task oriented with your current
   responsibilities   _____

   e. Remain patient   _____

2. DECIDE WHAT TO DELEGATE

   a. Delegate as much as possible   _____

   b. Delegate to the lowest level possible _____

   c. Take into consideration skill, workload,
   and interest of team members   _____

3. COMMUNICATE RESPONSIBILITIES TO TEAM MEMBERS

   a. Set goals (Specific, Measurable,
   Attainable, Relevant, Trackable)   _____

   b. Develop clear understanding of goals
   with team member   _____

   c. Define relative importance of the goals
   and task to the team member   _____

   d. Explain the potential complications   _____

   e. Stay results oriented, not procedure
   oriented   _____

   f. Set performance standards for the task
   (superior, good, and bad)   _____

   g. Communicate consequences of superior,
   good, and bad performance   _____

4. GRANT THE APPROPRIATE LEVEL OF AUTHORITY

   a. Determine which authority level team
   member is capable of handling
   (Levels A–D)   _____

    b. Notify others of the authority granted   _____

    c. Communicate the level of authority to the
       team member   _____

5. PROVIDE THE APPROPRIATE LEVEL OF SUPPORT

    a. Let team member know what available
       resources are   _____

    b. Give notice to others that the team
       member will be working with of the team
       member's new responsibilities   _____

    c. Communicate how much you will be
       available to help   _____

6. MONITOR THE DELEGATION

    a. Record current performance information   _____

    b. Provide sufficient levels of coaching to
       the team member   _____

    c. Enforce predetermined performance
       standards; communicate how team
       member is meeting those standards   _____

    d. Maintain open, objective communication
       with the team member   _____

    e. Give the team member opportunities to
       provide feedback on your delegation
       abilities during the task.   _____

7. EVALUATE THE DELEGATION

    a. Compare results of the task with the
       initial goals; why was or wasn't the
       delegation successful?   _____

    b. Evaluate team member's role during the
       delegation. Did he or she handle the level
       of authority granted? Could the person
       handle more authority next time? Were
       you disappointed? Evaluate team member
       on efficiency, timing, creativity,
       cooperation   _____

    c. Discuss your evaluation with team
       member   _____

    d. Provide team member with constructive
       criticism, both positive and negative
       feedback   _____

8. DID YOU ENCOUNTER ANY OF THE FOLLOWING
   PROBLEMS?

   a. Reverse delegation   _____

   b. Default decision making   _____

   c. Wrong purpose   _____

   d. Wrong person   _____

   e. Control system not accurate enough   _____

   f. Control system not specific enough   _____

   g. Control system biased   _____

Focus on the topics in this book that would be of most immediate benefit. Please consult the table of contents.

SUMMARY

The ability to effectively delegate is considered one of the most important skills of successful management. Effective delegation allows you to get your work done through others. It benefits you, your team members, and the organization as a whole. Effective delegation benefits you by promoting more cost-effective use of your time and increasing your promotion potential. Your team members increase their involvement in the projects they work on, develop new skills, and increase their promotion potential. From an organizational perspective, effective delegation promotes cost effectiveness, higher quality products, and increased flexibility.

Chapter Two

Why Managers Don't Delegate

Sally is a manager of administration for a manufacturing company and has 20 people working for her. Sally knows that delegation is important to being a successful manager. She delegates work to all her team members but still finds she doesn't have enough time to get her work done. It's Sunday night, and Sally decides she needs to sit down and prioritize all her responsibilities. She makes a list of priorities and on Monday goes to work feeling on top of the world, confident that she has a clear perspective of what needs to get done. Before Sally even reaches her office, however, one of Sally's employees, Jim, stops her with the greeting, "Sally, I am glad I caught you because *we* have a problem!!"

He goes on to quickly explain the nature of the crisis and the circumstances that led up to it, and then waits for Sally's response. Sally, seeing herself as a take-charge, problem-solving manager, replies, "This is an important problem; I'm glad you brought it to my attention. Let me consider the options and get back to you shortly." So before Sally even reaches her office, her one-day-old list of priorities is no longer relevant. She has just taken responsibility for Jim's problem and made it one of her highest priorities! Jim will do nothing more on the crisis until he hears from Sally.

Sally delegates tasks but not the responsibility and decision-making authority to complete them adequately.

Somewhere along the line, Sally acquired an inverted view of how managers should operate. Most problem-solving managers like Sally believe problems should be passed *up* the management chain instead of *down*. They think managers should be *responsible* and employees *responsive* to the managers. Laurie Johnston, controller for an East Coast manufacturer, sums up Sally's problem:

> Most managers I know are willing to delegate work tasks but insist on retaining control of the decision-making process. Their subordinates must continuously stop work to ask, "What should I do next?" They need permission to proceed or a decision about which alternative most pleases their boss to avoid second-guessing, criticism, and all the subtle, sometimes unconscious, ways managers make their workers feel powerless and look stupid."[1]

Sally needs to learn how to delegate decisions as well as tasks. She needs to be available to listen to her team members' problems, but she needs to encourage them to solve them on their own. Most employees want direction from the manager but are more highly motivated when they can make decisions on their own.

Sally's experience is not unique. Many managers do not delegate well. Although the ability to delegate is a basic managerial skill, studies indicate that delegation is often handled incorrectly.

Why? Part of the reason is that managers don't know how to delegate effectively. A larger reason, however, may be the fact that many managers don't want to delegate. For a number of reasons, they don't want to give up control in the work environment. They may equate control with power and feel that by giving up control they give up power. Or such a manager may be concerned with the perceptions of others and want other members of the organization to have visible indicators that he or she is "in charge." Constantly keeping employees waiting for an opinion or an approval might provide such outward appearances yet thinly veil underlying chaos. Such managers don't realize that they can exert power *through* their employees—and much more efficiently than if they attempt to do everything themselves.

Some managers need to be in control to ensure the job is done right—that is, the way *they* think it should be done! Other managers are inexperienced with delegation and afraid of its consequences. For example, Diane Hearing and Cheryl Smith, two hospital managers in Florida, both had common fears about the task of delegation:

> Diane Hearing, manager of the Coronary Care and Progressive Telemetry Unit of Morton Plan Hospital in Clearwater, Florida, remembers her fears when she contemplated delegating parts of her job. "By sharing responsibility, would I be admitting I couldn't handle my job?" was the question that haunted her. "I finally realized that I couldn't handle two departments, 60 staff members, and be a participative manager all by myself!"
>
> Cheryl Smith, manager of a 24-person intravenous therapy team serving 745-bed hospitals in Florida, started delegating when the unit needed a quality assurance program. "I felt it was too much for me to do, so I found a person on my staff who had worked in quality assurance before joining us. I felt guilty about asking her to take on additional work, but to my surprise, she was very willing." Smith meets periodically with the staff members to discuss progress. "We are still working on this project, but sharing makes so much difference," she says. "And I no longer feel that it's a sign of weakness if I don't do everything myself."[2]

Managers such as Diane Hearing, who are new to a position, fear being seen as inadequate. They need to rely heavily on the expertise of their team members and at the same time feel a need to maintain a front. Feelings of insecurity make them hesitant to delegate. Other managers like Cheryl Smith are afraid of appearing "bossy" and fear their team members will not accept new responsibilities.

Some experienced managers have a different problem. They become so focused on doing what needs to be done that they can't bear to delegate significant tasks to others. Mary Lou Fox, CEO of Westhaven Service Company, an institutional pharmacy based in Pettysburg, Ohio, is such an example. The company is so dependent on her doing everything, she is unable to leave her job! "If you pulled Mary Lou out of that company, it would fail," claims Lawrence Cryan, who recently served as controller for the firm. Over the years, Mary Lou made four distinct attempts to let go, bringing in outsiders and boosting insiders, resting her hopes on poised professional managers and then on eager trainees. But all attempts failed in large part due to Mary Lou's not knowing how to delegate. The difficulty was, she says, that nobody solved problems the way she would have solved them.[3]

EXCUSES MANAGERS MAKE

Managers who don't delegate have many reasons. Table 2–1 shows some of the excuses they give for not delegating a particular task.

MYTHS ABOUT DELEGATION

Managers believe a number of myths about delegation that hinder them from delegating effectively. Most of these myths derive from the manager's own fears—that team members can't get the job done right or will show the manager up and hinder the manager's career. Managers hinder their careers *only* by believing these myths.

TABLE 2–1
Excuses Managers Make for Not Delegating

---

1. My employees lack the experience.
2. It takes more time to explain than to do the job myself.
3. A mistake by an employee could be costly.
4. My position enables me to get quicker action.
5. There are some things I shouldn't delegate to anyone.
6. My employees are specialists, and they lack the overall knowledge that many decisions require.
7. My people are already too busy.
8. My employees just aren't ready to accept more responsibility.
9. I'm concerned about lack of control over my employee's performance when I delegate something to him or her.
10. I like keeping busy and making my own decisions.
11. Delegating is terrifying to me.

A manager can allay the fears and dispel the myths of delegation by learning and understanding the techniques of effective delegation described in this book.

Diminished Authority

Some managers believe that delegation diminishes their authority. They feel that their own power in the organization erodes when employees are given the power to achieve results. Such managers usually regard power as a limited resource. If an employee is given full power to spend money, for example, the manager perceives that his or her own power is diminished. The manager prefers to have the employee constantly check in for approval at each step of an assigned task to reinforce the manager's appearance as "the boss."

This notion of power is a misconception since the manager retains ultimate responsibility for the actions of all of his or her employees. Managers who have teams that perform well through effective delegation *increase* their own authority and power in an organization.

Lack of Confidence

Many managers lack confidence either in themselves or in their employees. Lack of confidence is another prime reason why many managers fail to delegate. Some managers don't trust employees to do a job or don't trust their own skills to effectively assign the task to an employee. Managers who lack confidence in their own abilities or in the abilities of their team members have three characteristics: (1) an aversion to taking risks, (2) a fear of appearing bossy, and (3) a fear of being shown up.

Aversion to risk. Managers who delegate take the risk that their employees might fail, and some managers are averse to risk. According to James Jenks and John Kelly, co-authors of *Don't Do. Delegate!:*

> The possibility of failure haunts some managers and to them seems a logical reason not to risk delegating. They think it's perfectly reasonable and right to be cautious. Since delegating requires them to give up some control and take calculated risks, these managers never delegate.[4]

Delegation encourages risk taking, and taking risks can have positive effects on an organization. Timothy Firnstahl, head of a $15 million restaurant company, describes one of his experiences with delegating:

> In one instance, our product developer and the chef of our newest restaurant had worked hard to adapt a lovely Mexican dish, prawns Veracruzana, for the restaurant. I opposed including it on the menu because it didn't fit our American cuisine image and reminded them that a clear theme is essential to a restaurant's success.

The chef and several others pointed out that the proposed offering was colorful, cost-effective, and delicious. Besides, why shortchange the guest because of a name? Good point. We came up with an American name, prawns piquant, put it on the menu, and the item is now a best-seller.[5]

Because of his openness to the suggestions of one of his key employees and confidence in that person's opinion, an idea Mr. Firnstahl may have quickly vetoed became a financial success for his business.

Effective delegators minimize risk by installing the proper controls for the particular situation. And delegation can be adapted to fit a variety of different situations; for example,

- A manager gives full responsibility and authority to a highly qualified team member to complete a task with no interference.
- Team members are given full authority to carry out tasks but are required to make regular progress reports so that management can coordinate their efforts with the work of others.
- With less-qualified team members, the manager retains approval on all decisions before any decision is carried out.
- A team member is assigned the task of presenting alternative solutions; the manager makes the final choice.[6]

Fear of being bossy. Many managers who lack confidence don't delegate because they are afraid of appearing bossy. But delegation has the opposite effect; it permits employees to participate in setting objectives and deciding how to get things done.

Fear of being shown up. Managers who lack confidence in their abilities or in their position are afraid that their employees will show them up. Such managers fail to realize that their own performance depends on the performance of their team members. A manager's competence is a function of the competence of the team members. Successful managers take pride in the superior performance of their team members. Good managers also take advantage of competent employees and delegate increasing amounts of responsibility to them.

Retained Visibility

Some managers retain as many tasks as possible, especially the important ones that are visible to upper management. They want others in the organization—especially those above them—to see their achievements, and they believe such visibility will increase their chances of promotion.

Some managers gain a sense of importance by doing as much work as possible or completing the assignments they deem important. The important assignments may involve special kinds of decisions or contact with individuals who are higher in the organization. These managers need to reevaluate their roles. Obviously, some crucial decisions should be made by the manager. Unfortunately, some managers view *every* decision as crucial and as a result want to make them all. Such managers put forth a facade when they ask others to do a task. They are going through the motions but not really delegating.

For example, *Management Solutions* describes a purchasing manager who delegated a task but left no room for individual initiative:

> . . . one purchasing manager delegated the task of purchasing a certain line of items to his assistant. The manager then proceeded to overrule every purchase plan the assistant developed until the plan eventually conformed to the way the purchasing manager would have drawn it up himself in the first place. Although this manager genuinely believed

that he was delegating, he was actually confusing "nominal" delegation with "real" delegation.[7]

Managers who guard their power and delegate sparingly fail to develop their successors and thereby limit their own advancement. Such an approach robs them of the exposure gained by having a staff of successful, well-trained employees. Such employees give managers visibility by being one of their people. It's just as beneficial to have an executive comment: "That's one of Sally's direct reports—we know he's been well trained."

Lack of Time

Many managers complain that it takes too much time to effectively delegate assignments, especially if the employee is new or the assignment is complex or in some way sensitive. Sometimes time is lacking because managers have not appropriately planned and scheduled activities that need to be done. In this case, the manager might make personal last-minute efforts to save projects, and thus think he or she is a hero to the department. At other times, a manager is unwilling to take the necessary time to work with or train an employee to do a task properly.

Lack of time might be a legitimate roadblock for delegating in the short term. In the long term, however, delegation saves the manager time when a similar task needs to be completed again. Delegation also develops employees who are able to do a wider range of tasks on shorter notice and strengthens the manager-employee relationship.

Lack of Familiarity

An increasing number of managers don't delegate because they fear or don't understand new technologies. An actuarial manager unfamiliar with computers might prefer to make calculations by hand rather than delegate the task to a computer services specialist. Some managers are unfamiliar with other areas of the organization. The manager may not delegate a problem to a corporate staff function because the manager never met anyone from the department. The manager is unaware of how the department could help.

Individual Habit

If a manager has been doing the same task for many years, he or she may continue to handle the responsibility simply out of habit. Many managers are committed to writing out all correspondence by hand versus dictating or assigning the task to an assistant. Others maintain their own files, type notes, and answer their own phone because they have always done such activities and are comfortable doing them. These poor habits, however, are bound to make the manager less effective than he or she might otherwise be.

MYTHS ABOUT SUCCESS IN AN ORGANIZATION

Many managers believe three basic myths about success in an organization: the superworker myth, the perfectionist myth, and the replacement myth. These myths are at the root of the problem of ineffective delegation. Understand and guard against these myths in your own management practices.

The Superworker Myth

Many managers don't delegate because they want to be seen as superworkers. These managers believe they have to prove themselves to others. They may have a martyr

FIGURE 2–1
Three Myths about Success in an Organization

The Superworker Myth

The Perfectionist Myth

The Replacement Myth

complex or a larger than average ego. A superworker enjoys having the reputation of being hardworking and often will be sure to work more hours than anyone else in the department. These workaholics take pride in being constantly busy. They seldom use their time efficiently or effectively, however, and usually overextend themselves so that nothing ends up done quite right. They never have time to do a task correctly but always seem to be able to find time to do it over. A typical comment from such an individual is: "I'll finish this report, I was going to come in this weekend anyway."

Insecure managers who need to have a reason to feel important or justify their positions often subscribe to the superworker myth. Constant activity gives them a reason. If a manager works harder and longer than anyone else in the department, so the myth goes, he surely must be more valuable to the organization than others. Hence, the manager is justified in having the position. Such managers focus too much on appearances rather than responsibilities. They tend to be overly concerned with what others think rather than with the results being produced.

A superworker fails to realize that most employees resent this style. Sooner or later, the person establishes a reputation as an ineffective manager who is always busy yet often doing the wrong things. Superworkers are often rudely surprised when their career path is blocked. Upper management realizes such individuals can't handle higher levels of responsibility, which require managing a greater number of tasks and people.

The Perfectionist Myth

A related reason work is not effectively delegated is the adage, "If you want something done right, do it yourself." Perfectionists pay special attention to the details of every assignment and expect to have everything perfect. They sincerely believe they can do most tasks better than any of their employees—and they probably can. The perfectionist may trust an unimportant job to an employee if it doesn't have to be done "just right." Important tasks or those that will be seen by someone higher in the organization will be completed by the perfectionist personally. A typical comment: "Let me double-check these accounting figures—I want to be certain there are no errors."

A perfectionist attitude disguises a lack of trust in employees and in their ability to do assigned work. Moreover, most tasks can be accomplished in a number of different ways; the manager doesn't have the only acceptable way. Sometimes managers who defend this myth cite examples when employees were trusted with an assignment and failed to complete it properly. Their bad experience in the past limits their enthusiasm about delegating further assignments. The perfectionist manager fears that mistakes made by the employees reflect on his or her competence. Such a manager usually feels that control is lost once a task is delegated. For this manager, the only alternative when a task is done incorrectly is to either reassign the task or do it over personally.

Managers who fall into this category fail to realize that there is often more than one way to do something right and that there are a number of ways to monitor the performance of employees no matter how the assignment is undertaken. The manager may know a way to complete a certain task that has worked well in the past or have an inkling of what his or her manager wants to see in the finished product. The manager then seeks to impose insights on the employee in a way that dampens the employee's enthusiasm for the project—or worse—gives the employee absolutely no latitude.

This approach undermines employees' creativity and denies the possibility that other methods might be just as effective in achieving the desired results. This type of manager usually fails to understand both his role as a manager and the techniques for effective delegation. Not all assignments need to be done perfectly—most have a latitude for error. An assignment seldom has to be done the manager's way to be effectively completed. Managers can interject their or their manager's, preferences for how the project could be completed without dictating how the task must be done.

The Replacement Myth

Some managers don't delegate because they're afraid of being replaced by an employee who does a great job. At the very least, such managers claim overachieving employees will expect to be paid more for taking on additional responsibilities. Such a view is shortsighted. And such managers aren't doing their jobs adequately—that is, obtaining the greatest results with the available resources. Word about the true nature of the situation quickly gets around the organization. Sooner or later, the talents of good employees will be seen, and the manager will lose credibility as a result. Good employees will most likely leave the company, a serious loss for the organization. Some managers justify their delegation shortcomings with comments such as: "If I give you more responsibilities, people will think I'm playing favorites."

A manager who fears being shown up by an employee does not realize that good performance by an employee is a credit to the manager. Indeed, when an employee performs well, the manager is viewed as having good judgment in selecting and training the employee. The employee is seen as bringing positive visibility to the manager's area. In addition to becoming more accomplished as a manager, the effective delegator prepares employees to one day take his or her own job. With this strategy, the manager can have a replacement ready when an opportunity for promotion arises.

THE DIFFICULT MOVE FROM EMPLOYEE TO MANAGER

Anyone who achieves the move from employee to manager does so through a combination of individual ambition and competence. The job of managing is no different. Practically everyone in an organization is initially hired for specific technical abilities or functional skills. As they excel at those skills, they are given greater responsibility. Most likely, promotion to a managerial position follows. As an employee moves from worker to manager, he or she must shift from doer to supervisor. This transition involves a shift from using a specific set of skills to using skills in human interaction as shown in Figure 2–2.

Even those individuals who don't want to be managers need to know how to effectively delegate. In almost any position, a person is called on to assign work to others: administrative assistants, technical support personnel, and fellow project members must all be delegated to from time to time.

Once a person moves from a technical or specialized position to a management position, the person must shift focus from individual achievement to achievement through a group. The main way to accomplish this shift is through the skill of delegating. What becomes more important is not what the manager can do but what he or she can do through others. This often difficult transition is crucial for new managers to have enough time to complete their managerial tasks.

For example, a top salesperson is promoted to a management position in charge of other sales representatives. In this position, she is no longer able to perform the task she does best, namely, selling. Instead, the new position takes her away from direct customer contact, and she is forced to do primarily administrative work—a task that she always hated. She may resist her new role by continuing to contact customers and maintain business ties,

FIGURE 2-2
Skills Needed, Team Members and Managers

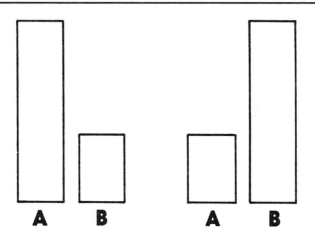

A = Technical skills: accounting, sales,
       engineering, legal, electronics, researching,
       etc.
B = Human interaction skills: delegating,
       communicating, negotiating, discussing,
       confronting, giving feedback

although this activity is now supposed to be her employees' responsibility.

In another case, an engineer is so good at solving technical problems that he's promoted to the position of manager. Whenever a difficult technical problem comes up in
the department, the new manager enjoys rolling up his
sleeves and digging in. He feels that doing this gives him
the chance to demonstrate his wide range of abilities to
everyone in the department. What he fails to realize, however, is that such technical work makes a serious dent in
his limited time and many of his management tasks are
suffering. In addition, his direct involvement in technical

problems keeps others in the department from working on the most challenging assignments and denies them the chance to learn and grow. In fact, the employees view such difficult problems as the most exciting part of their jobs, and they resent the manager's intrusion.

A third example is the shift an entrepreneur of a startup company must make to become a manager of a mature organization. Most successful entrepreneurs are driven by a strong desire to start and build a new product or concept. They excel at promoting the idea and pulling together and motivating a qualified team of individuals to make the idea a reality. Once they succeed, however, running a mature company often requires a completely different set of skills. There is more emphasis on monitoring activities and less on creation and pursuit of new idea. This shift often bores or frustrates the true entrepreneur. The company is frequently better off if the entrepreneur sells out, and a new management team is brought in with the skills needed to run an already successful organization.

Some magnetism draws new managers to those activities in which they previously excelled. They're good at such tasks, and they can accomplish them quickly—much faster than anyone still learning the skill. They have a strong desire to continue acting the superstar, a role they were previously praised for.

Even a skilled and talented manager must rely on others' knowledge and abilities, especially as she climbs higher in the organization. Available time is limited, and even with the best effort, a manager's perspective in the organization is narrow. The manager needs to shift focus from *being* an individual expert to *relying* on individual experts who can achieve both the manager's goals and those of the department and organization.

Of course managers should pitch in occasionally to help their employees get a job done. Such assistance can go a long way toward building group morale and a team atmosphere. However, even when a manager does help out, such assistance should not be crucial to successfully accomplish the task. The manager's assistance should be a symbolic activity that demonstrates his or her support for the group and the goal.

OVERCOMING EMPLOYEE RESISTANCE TO DELEGATION

A major reason many managers find it difficult to delegate is that some employees don't want to accept delegation. For various reasons, the employee has the ability to do an assignment but elects not to accept or complete it. Some of the reasons an employee may resist an assignment include no incentive, no training, avoidance of responsibility, fearfulness and uncertainty, feeling that the task is not part of the job description, and distrust of either the manager or the organization.

No Incentive

A predominant reason many employees fail to do an assigned activity is lack of a sufficient incentive. For them, the level of reward is not equal to the level of time, energy, and risk required. There may be no negative consequences for either not doing the job or not doing it well. Although the task may be a part of the job, many assignments can be completed haphazardly. As the manager, you must provide adequate positive and (when necessary) negative incentives to get the best effort possible from each employee.

Many times employees' motivation will increase if they are involved in planning and decision making for the task. If a task is not properly delegated, employees won't be involved making the decision or planning the activity.

Employees then have little commitment to the task. Employees need to feel ownership of any task they're working on for you to obtain their best efforts. Employees should be part of planning and decision making, especially if the decisions affect them or their work.

Involvement in an assignment should take place as soon as practical. For specific tasks, tell an employee what approaching tasks will need to be completed. This way, the employee has an idea of the type and size of future assignments. He or she is then better prepared to accept the tasks when you assign them.

For more general areas of responsibility, you have greater freedom to involve employees. You can have employees generate a list of tasks that need to be done in each area or conduct periodic discussions with each employee about job responsibilities and expectations. You can solicit employees' opinions prior to making a decision that will affect specific or general job responsibilities in the department. If possible, have assignments coincide with each employee's desire for skill enhancement and career development.

No Training

Many times a manager asks employees to handle tasks they haven't been trained to do. "What we could really use to make this decision more easily is a sales forecast. Dan, could you put one together?" Rather than risk appearing stupid, Dan may stumble through the assignment with much stress and delay, ask a peer for assistance, or spend time frantically searching through a library for helpful resources. The finished work doesn't meet the manager's expectations and may be completely unacceptable. This scenario can be avoided with good communication and proper training. Try serving as the trainer and providing one-on-one direction and support. Or send the employee to a seminar on the skill area.

Avoidance of Responsibility

Most employees realize that if they can avoid making a major decision concerning a task, they can also avoid responsibility for the task, hence making for an easier, less stressful job. At the same time, since most managers enjoy making decisions, they tend to be naturally receptive to making decisions for the employee. The result of these two tendencies is an employee who does not learn to make decisions and live with their consequences and a manager who is not truly delegating. For these reasons, be sure the employee makes a commitment and accepts accountability for delegated work.

Fearfulness and Uncertainty

An employee who wants to be certain of pleasing the manager seeks approval of all activities he or she plans prior to and during the completion of a task. In an attempt to please the manager, the employee completes the task precisely as requested, including arriving at the results the manager hoped to obtain. If the task involves a recommendation, for example, the employee provides the answer the manager wants to hear, regardless of whether it's the best solution. The employee isn't thinking and acting independently.

The employee is satisfied with providing a solution well received by the manager and being protected from the possibility of error. If the solution turns out to be a poor one, he was only following the manager's instructions, and thus only the manager should be blamed. A manager who tells an employee how to proceed with each step of the task has failed to delegate the activity.

You must encourage insecure employees to assume responsibility. Jenks and Kelly state that managers who have these type of employees need to ask themselves the following questions:

- Do I really talk about results I want rather than methods?
- Do I discourage my people when they ask for advice they don't really need?
- Do I turn back their questions to them, forcing them to tell me what course they'll take before I comment?
- Do I take back tasks too quickly before making every effort to keep the team member accountable?[8]

Not Their Job

Some employees think when they accept responsibility for an assigned task they are doing the manager's or some other employee's job. Try to elicit and discuss such feelings when you make an assignment. Persuade the employee to make a commitment to the task. For example, you can change the employee's job description to specifically make the task part of her responsibilities. If an employee doesn't want to do a job because it's mundane and distasteful, consider rotating the assignment among employees.

Distrust of the Manager or the Organization

If an employee believes the manager will take credit for the work he or she does, or if the manager has the habit of changing or reworking all completed assignments, the employee will be reluctant to accept or complete tasks. If this is the case, the manager may need to do a self-assessment to uncover the reason for the employee's reluctance. Where distrust is valid, the manager and employee must develop a plan for working together.

Even if an employee does trust her manager, sometimes she does not trust other people or policies in the organization. Employees who act inappropriately may damage their career and future prospects with the organization. For example, if a manager assigns a task that is politically unpopular in the organization, an employee who completes the assignment may alienate himself from other people in the firm.

Be sensitive to your employees' attitudes about delegation. Where problems exist, discuss the delegation process with employees. In this way, you can reach an understanding and delegate assignments effectively with minimal chances for misunderstanding.

SUMMARY

Effective managers come to grips with the risks, real or imagined, involved in delegation. They learn to delegate in a way that is comfortable both for them and for their employees. They discuss with employees any concerns about getting the job done. They do whatever possible to help employees complete assigned tasks—without doing the assignments for them.

If you're reluctant to delegate, be honest with yourself. If your reason involves a lack of know-how, read on. If you just prefer not to delegate, weigh the advantages and disadvantages against your personal and professional objectives. You can achieve far more if you delegate effectively.

Chapter Three

Preparing to Delegate

Delegation is not as simple as asking an employee "Would you do this task for me?" It requires thoughtful preparation. Sam, a project manager at a consulting firm, found this out when he started delegating. Sam worked very hard to achieve the position of project manager. He gave his maximum effort to all the projects he was responsible for. Sam felt he was doing his best when he was able to help a client by successfully completing a project while at the same time making money for his company. Sam enjoyed doing his best! For each new project, Sam's personal standards compelled him to make his best effort. Sam was satisfied with his method of operation, and everyone he was involved with was pleased with the consistent level and quality of his work.

Although this method worked well for Sam, he knew that, to get promoted again, he had to train and trust other people to do tasks he knew he could do himself. Training even the brightest, most energetic employees was a frustrating activity. Sam felt uncomfortable slowing down the pace to make sure the members of his team did things right. When Sam first started delegating and training new team members, he viewed the activity as a hindrance.

Fortunately, Sam learned to redefine delegation as an *investment* in a person for the future, rather than a means of getting a single task done at a particular point in time. Once Sam adopted this philosophy about training new team members, delegation became much easier for him. He gained a new perspective on the activity. It was still difficult for Sam to delegate at first, but he saw the fruits of his labor within weeks. The trained employee carried more responsibilities—tasks Sam used to think only he could do right. The positive experience made Sam more willing to take the time to delegate to other team members.

Delegation depends on many variables: the environment, the type of job, the experience of the employee, the timing of the situation, and the length of the manager and employee's working relationship.

Three essential steps in preparing to delegate include:

- Developing the right attitudes.
- Deciding what to delegate.
- Deciding who to delegate to.

DEVELOPING THE RIGHT ATTITUDES

As Sam discovered, to be truly effective at delegating, you must have the right attributes and attitudes about delegation. These positive attributes, outlined below, include personal security, risk taking, a trusting nature, task orientation, and a good degree of patience.

Personal Security

Managers who are good at delegating feel confident in their abilities and position in the company and have a positive attitude about delegating. They consider delegating a means to prepare team members to be future managers. They view delegation as a means of achieving their own, and the company's, performance goals.

Risk Taking

Good delegators are willing to take risks to get tasks done, stretching resources and making mistakes. They are willing to accept and learn from failure. They must allow both less experienced and more knowledgeable employees to make decisions.

Trusting Nature

Good delegators are willing to trust another to perform a task for which they alone will be held responsible. They grant such trust with full knowledge of any limitations the team members may have, such as a lack of experience. They allow the team member to supply, without interference, his own ideas as to how an assignment should be completed. They don't revoke their trust after an assignment is completed. Team members need to be supported even if the actions they take are criticized by others. For example, if a person is given authority to conduct an audit, that person should be supported regardless of the audit's finding.

The following general guidelines help increase team members' trust.

Backstop team members' decisions.   Even though you don't agree with team members' decisions, back them up when they need support, especially in front of others.

Don't harp on team members' mistakes.   Team members usually realize when they make a mistake. Don't dwell on mistakes. Give employees the opportunity to correct them.

Don't spy on team members.   Set clear guidelines for monitoring progress that are known to each team member. Stick to the agreed-on guidelines, and don't spy on team members to determine their progress.

Don't withhold information as a test.   Withholding useful information leads employees to mistrust you and your motives.

Be open. Don't try to hide your own mistakes from team members. Freely share information necessary for a team member to perform her job.

Clarify expectations. Share your expectations with team members—in advance.

Show respect. Treat team members with respect and courtesy.

Don't manipulate. Be straightforward in the delegation of tasks. Don't manipulate employees with guilt or implied rewards.

Examine assumptions. Make sure you are making valid assumptions. For example, if a team member resists performing a task, don't immediately assume the employee is looking for the easiest way out.[1]

Task Orientation

Effective delegation establishes and employs a means of control including channels (progress reports, review sessions, etc.) for reporting progress and problems as well as a schedule for when reporting should take place (daily, weekly, monthly, etc.). If you aren't comfortable with the amount of feedback and the level of control, establish means for additional monitoring. If you are especially concerned about a particular assignment, tell the team member that you are going to follow up frequently on the project's progress. Such warning helps to buffer any feelings of meddling.

When necessary, be willing to intervene and hold team members accountable for their action or lack of action. You can redirect team members' efforts, give them additional authority to complete the assignment, or take back the assignment if the satisfactory completion is doubtful. Accountability must extend to the completed assignment. If the assignment is done poorly, reprimand the responsible team member. Adjust future assignments so the team member gets smaller, less significant tasks until he or she once again demonstrates willingness and competence to assume greater responsibility.

Ample Patience

A manager who is a good delegator realizes that results take time. She can see what needs to be done but doesn't order it done a specific way. She is willing to allow team members the chance to develop judgment by letting them try in their own methods. If a project falls behind schedule, the manager makes certain the team member has a plan for meeting the deadline; the manager doesn't panic and take over the project. The manager must allow time for delegation. She must allow time for assignment of specific tasks as well as for inexperienced employees to be trained.

In summary, as Thomas R. Horton, former CEO of the American Management Association, says: "The process of delegation must begin by a spark of faith. Kindled by accomplishment, it is ultimately sustained by trust. Effective delegators are the managers who believe in their people as much as in themselves and who know that from that belief comes not just accomplishment, but growth."[2]

DECIDING WHAT TO DELEGATE

Once you have the right attitude about delegation, the next step in the delegation process is deciding what work can and should be delegated. Managers often don't know what activities and assignments to delegate. A good manager delegates as much as possible—of the right tasks. The trick is to delegate what you do understand, not what you don't. Even if you have time to do a task, consider assigning it to a team member if the team member is capable of assuming the responsibility.

The following technique will help determine which tasks need to be delegated.

- Draw up a list of current job responsibilities that you would leave behind if you were to suddenly leave your job.
- Next, list the team members qualified to take over each of those responsibilities. If there is no one ready to take over a responsibility, leave a blank space.
- When the list is complete, add up the blank spaces to see what kind of a department you would leave if you were suddenly out of the picture.
- Are you satisfied with the results?[3]

Whenever possible, delegate an entire task. Delegating an entire task increases a team member's initiative, gives you more control over the results, minimizes confusion, and eliminates unnecessary and inefficient coordination among team members. By delegating an entire task, you can devote more time to management activities, such as supervising team members and coordinating work to be completed.

Overdelegating is seldom a problem, especially if an adequate control system is developed. Projects too large to delegate to a single person should be divided into segments manageable for one individual. One way to do this is to write down all tasks that need to be done and then answer the following questions. Which tasks require different skills and abilities? Can each task be completed in the amount of time the job is expected to take? Can results be achieved in a timely and efficient manner? If not,

FIGURE 3–1
What to Delegate

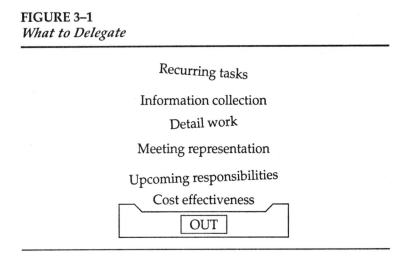

divide the task further and assign to more individuals. Think the various tasks through to be sure they make sense.

A variety of factors need to be considered when deciding what tasks to delegate including employee abilities and interests, the type and nature of the tasks, and their relation to upcoming responsibilities.

What Should be Delegated

General qualifications for the type of work to delegate include the following.

- The task can be handled adequately by team members.
- All necessary information for decision making is available to team members.
- The task involves operational detail rather than planning or organization.

- The task does not require skills unique to you or your position.
- An individual other than you has, or can have, direct control over the task.[4]

Specific types of tasks to delegate include the following.

Recurring tasks. If an assignment is likely to recur and it requires technical or mechanical skills, it makes sense to delegate the activity to a team member. This way, one individual becomes the expert on that activity and can handle the task faster and more efficiently. If the task is boring and needs to be done over an extended period of time, it's best to rotate the responsibility to different individuals.

Information collection. Doing research in a library or searching for information in company files is a job you can easily delegate. Assignments to collect information firsthand from throughout the organization, from customers, or from outside experts can also be delegated.

Detail work. Delegate assignments that involve excessive details and minor decision making, such as calculations. Usually these type of tasks have very little direct impact on the results you're trying to achieve and rarely require your skills. These tasks can take up a great deal of your time without producing significant results.

Meeting representation. Delegate team members to attend meetings on your behalf. Depending on the purpose, team members may openly participate and represent you in this capacity. After attending the meeting, team members can relay any issues of importance to you or report them at staff meetings.

Upcoming responsibilities. Delegate activities that will be a part of the team members' future responsibilities. If a reorganization of responsibilities is planned, for example, start assigning tasks that team members will be required to do afterward. If a team member aspires to another position, assign tasks that he or she would do in the other job.

Cost effectiveness. Delegate activities that would be more economically performed by a team member. Determine a cost effective approach by identifying your tasks and responsibilities, determining which can be delegated, and delegating them to the lowest level possible.

What Should Not Be Delegated

Certain activities should not be delegated because they are either specific managerial tasks or tasks that are proprietary in nature. Tasks that should not be delegated include the task of delegating, employee evaluations, employee discipline, counseling, planning, confidential tasks, specific assignments from the manager's manager, complex situations, and situations involving sensitive issues. These tasks are discussed below.

Delegation process. Don't assign the delegation process itself to someone else. Any work that is to be conducted by your direct team members should be delegated and explained by you. Any other arrangement inevitable leads to communication errors.

Performance evaluations. Performance evaluations, for an assignment or an annual appraisal, are a managerial responsibility. Tasks that are delegated to a team member should not be evaluated by someone else. The evaluation usually depends on the initial discussion

FIGURE 3–2
What not to Delegate

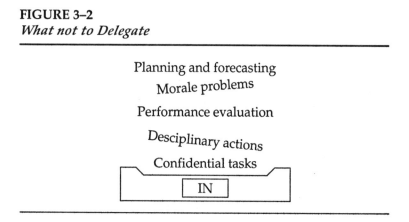

of the assignment and mutually agreed-on standards and expectations.

Disciplinary actions. When you discipline a team member, do it privately and only after you know all the facts. Some managers tend to avoid all unpleasant aspects of their job, and disciplining team members is a responsibility very few managers enjoy. Disciplinary action is, nonetheless, a necessary part of any managerial position. Giving the task to someone else diminishes the effectiveness of the message—and of the manager. Most team members who receive criticism secondhand are bothered by the fact it wasn't personally communicated by you.

Counseling and morale problems. Counseling a team member whose performance or attitude is unacceptable is another difficult management task. Such a task, like disciplinary action, needs to be done by you in private. Employee counseling is part of your job that cannot be done by someone else.

Planning and forecasting. Some of the detail work involved in planning and forecasting, such as calculations and research, can be delegated. The conceptual part of the planning and forecasting cannot. Decide how the department's goals fit into the overall goals of the organization. You alone are in the best position to make that decision.

Confidential tasks. Don't delegate activities that involve sensitive or classified information, such as salaries, unless such work is a specific part of the person's job. Base assignments on the need for team members to know specific sensitive information. Once a task is classified as sensitive, perform the task yourself or delegate it to an appropriate individual. When this is not possible, divide the task into segments so the whole assignment is not readily discernible.

Specifically assigned tasks. Don't delegate activities that are purposely assigned to you by your manager. If your manager specifically requests that you complete a certain activity because he or she wants to know your opinion, for example, it is inappropriate to reassign the task to someone else.

Complex situations. If a situation is so confusing that you don't clearly understand it yourself, don't expect a team member to be able to handle it. You may not know how significant a problem is until you first learn more about it yourself. Only when you know and understand the boundaries of the problem are you able to divide and delegate roles. Delegating a poorly understood task is ineffective; team members will be refered back to you for clarification.

Sensitive situations. Don't delegate activities that are sensitive, such as resolving a political conflict or requesting sensitive information from elsewhere in the organization. The team member is not in the best position to complete such an assignment. It is awkward for you to place someone in such a role.

DECIDING WHO TO DELEGATE TO

Selecting people for various work assignments is one of the most important skills in effective delegation. Of course, managers are limited by the quality of the people in the work group, so it is important to hire the best individuals possible when opportunities arise. What skills, knowledge, or abilities are needed to perform various tasks? Of the tasks that need to be completed, who is interested in each?

Factors Affecting Selection

Three factors are of primary importance in the selection of the right person for an assignment: demonstrated skill, employee interest, and employee workload.

Demonstrated skill. Who is capable of completing the assignment? It's helpful to know the team members' record on similar assignments. Although not practical with new employees, strive to find out the employee's work record. In addition, have a feel for how well the person works with others, in which situations the person operates best, and the person's ability to work under pressure. The person's skill level doesn't need to exceed the requirements of the task. It doesn't make sense, for example, to use the most experienced computer programmer to write a simple program. Such an assignment is likely to frustrate or bore the programmer who is capable of more difficult assignments. If no one in the work group is capable of doing the assignment, consider training someone to do the task. Who could be trained to handle the assignment? How long would such training take?

Employee motivation. The employee's motivation and intent are as important as his or her ability. To best determine team member interest in a task, you need a working knowledge of the professional interests and goals of each employee in the group. When prior knowledge is not possible, this is a good opportunity to involve team members in the delegation process. Speak with them and determine the activities they are interested in and the goals they feel are reasonable for the department. Even if you don't agree with or use the input obtained, the employee contributes to the process and thus is more willing to accept the delegation when it occurs. Of course, an activity can still be assigned to a team member even if he or she has no interest in the task. However, first consideration should be given to those individuals highly interested in and motivated by the assignment.

Employee workload. Besides assessing ability and motivation, you need to decide if the team member has the time available to assume another assignment. How much is she currently doing? How well is she handling the assignments she has? How does her workload compare to that of others in the department?

Effective delegation does not necessarily involve an even division of tasks and responsibilities. Some people enjoy being delegated to more than others, and some are better at doing assigned tasks. Most team members realize they earn advancement only through work and achievements. Their level of interest in receiving delegation often serves as a barometer for their level of ambition. More ambitious workers are usually quite willing to take

FIGURE 3–3
Match Tasks with People

on heavier workloads and may even initiate tasks that need to be done. Encourage such attitudes.

Matching Tasks and People

Using knowledge about the person's abilities and the nature and difficulty of the task, determine the potential for success for the given assignment. Does the team member's skills match the needs of the assignment? Is the team member motivated to accept the assignment and do quality work? Do the team members have the potential for advancement? Selecting the right person for the task can be tricky. If given the chance, many people do very well at activities they never previously attempted.

The best person to get an assignment may not be the most skillful or experienced. The employee's current level of work and his or her availability should influence your decision as well. The employee needs to have enough time available. Keep in mind, however, that many managers believe the busiest person is often best at efficiently organizing his or her time to take on more work.

Given these variables, what is the best means of achieving the overall goals of the department? Are team members being encouraged to take individual initiative and accept greater responsibility? Are those employees who do seek additional responsibility being rewarded and recognized? Answering such questions will help you prepare for effective delegation.

A more formal decision model for determining what to delegate can be found in the Appendix.

SUMMARY

Effective delegation requires careful preparation. Three steps are important when preparing to delegate: (1) develop the right attitudes, (2) decide what and what not to delegate, and (3) decide who to delegate to. The "right" attitudes about delegation include personal security, willingness to take risk, willingness to trust team members, task orientation, and patience.

The second step in preparing to delegate is deciding what to delegate. Delegate any task that can be adequately handled by team members and does not require skills unique to your position. Examples of tasks that should be delegated include recurring tasks, information collection, detail work, and representation at meetings. Examples of tasks that should not be delegated include performance evaluations, disciplinary actions, counseling and morale problems, planning and forecasting, and sensitive situations.

The third step in preparing to delegate is deciding who to delegate to. When deciding who to delegate to, consider each team member's demonstrated skill level, interest, and workload.

Chapter Four

The Task of Delegating

Effective communication is the heart of delegation. Unfortunately, as in all human interaction, communication is easily misconstrued. Sally knows that delegation is important to being a successful manager. From experience, she also knows that delegation is a difficult task. She remembers her frustration when she recently gave an assignment to a new employee. Sally was determined not to badger the person about the task because she wanted to show that she trusted him. Since she wanted to allow him the space to work independently, she avoided checking up to see if the work was being done correctly.

As the deadline drew near, Sally casually asked him how the project was coming. She was distraught to find out that he hadn't yet started. In a panic, she took back the assignment and did the task herself, working overtime and most of two weekends to finish by the due date. This experience left Sally wary about delegating future assignments. It reinforced her bias that you can't trust others to do a job right. Sally was sure she would never again delegate something she considered really important.

What went wrong? Was the employee incompetent, irresponsible, or just unable to work autonomously? More likely this was a case of poor delegation. When Sally assigned the task, the assignment was clear to her. The employee, however, did not understand what was required—in this case, the importance of completing the task on time. Perhaps Sally didn't express the importance of the time element. Perhaps she said the right words but they somehow didn't register with the employee. In either case, the delegation failed. Although Sally and the employee may both be to blame, it is Sally who suffers the consequences.

Sally's problem is one that could be solved with additional experience in delegating . . . if she knows what to watch for and correct. As mentioned earlier, many managers fail to delegate not because they don't want to but because they don't know how to.

Effective delegation is more than simply telling or asking someone to do something. The task needs to be properly presented. The delegation process is a mutual consultation and agreement between you and your team members. Solicit team members' reactions and ideas any time during the process to establish the trust, support, and open communication necessary for obtaining best results. Explain *why* an assignment needs to be done, not just *what* needs to be done.

Essential steps for effective delegation include:

- Clearly communicate to team members what they are being asked to do.
- Provide context and relevance for the assignment.
- Clearly communicate the performance standards by which the team member will be evaluated.
- Make sure the team member has enough authority to complete the task.
- Communicate the level of support for the delegated task.
- Obtain obligation and commitment from the team member for the delegated task.

- Establish rewards for the team member's performance.

You must complete all these steps to effectively delegate a task. The scope of the assignment, however, determines to what extent each step is completed. A large responsibility requires a plan for each step; a small task may not need as much detail. By completing all these steps you ensure that the team member knows what to do, has enough authority and information to accomplish the task, and is held accountable. Leaving any of the steps out leads to frustration and dissatisfaction.

Following is a more detailed look at the essentials of delegating a task: communicating responsibilities, setting performance standards, providing authority, communicating the level of support the team members will receive, obtaining obligation and commitment from team members, and establishing a reward system.

COMMUNICATING RESPONSIBILITIES

First and foremost, you must make sure team members understand the responsibilities they are assuming. The responsibilities may be specific or general, written or oral, and cover a brief or extended period of time. The more specific the responsibilities, the better the odds that the task will be completed as intended. It is often impossible to identify exactly what needs to be done. For example, if you assign the task of assisting customers with problems, the best solution is not likely to be known until specific problems surface. In such instances, you are actually delegating a situation, not a task. The first step in assigning responsibilities is to agree on goals and objectives of the task with the team member.

Setting Goals

Paul Hersey, Ken Blanchard, and Scott Myers emphasize the importance of setting goals with an analogy to bowling:

> . . when they approach the alley, they notice there are no pins at the other end; that is, they don't know what their goals are. How long would you want to bowl without any pins? Yet every day in the world of work, people are bowling without any pins, and as a result cannot tell how well they are doing.[1]

Explain both the overall goals of the task as well as the specific goals related to the team member. A delegated task won't be carried out properly if you don't clearly outline its purpose. By answering the following questions, you can determine and communicate specific goals.

- What specifically needs to be done?
- When does the task need to be completed?
- What are the consequences of the task not being completed on time?
- What level of accuracy is needed in completing the task?
- How does the task fit into the overall scheme of things?
- How many parts are there to the entire project?
- Who else is working on those parts?

Hersey and Blanchard state that effective goals are SMART (Specific, Measurable, Attainable, Relevant, Trackable).

Goals must be SPECIFIC. Don't simply tell a team member to complete a study. Specify what to study as well as any alternatives for completing the study. Set milestones for completing the study.

FIGURE 4–1
Good Goals Are SMART Goals

Specific
Measurable
Attainable
Relevant
Trackable

Goals must be MEASURABLE. If you can't measure it, the team member can't manage it. Set goals that are observable and measurable.

Goals must be ATTAINABLE. Team members need to be able to reach their goals, learning and expanding their skills in the process. In general, high achievers like to set moderately difficult but obtainable goals.

Goals must be RELEVANT. Limit the number of goals and concentrate on setting goals in areas that are important to the task. This helps the team member know what is important for the task.

Goals must be TRACKABLE. Set interim goals so the team member can get feedback along the way. A goal is a destination, and you must manage the journey. If you delegate a task of developing a report, you have a much better chance of receiving an acceptable report if you require interim reports.[2]

PROVIDE CONTEXT AND RELEVANCE

Communicate not only what needs to be done but *why* it needs to be done. Answering the following questions helps you determine and communicate the overall goals of a task:

- Why is it important to have the task completed?
- Why does it need to be completed by the given deadline?
- What context surrounds the assignment?
- A task has more meaning to an employee when the surrounding circumstances are known.

Relative Importance

When assigning responsibilities for a task, explain the level of priority for the assignment and how it fits into the overall operations of the department. This discussion should explain the background of the assignment and all events and problems leading up to it. A crucial assignment requires greater care in implementation, closer attention to detail, and a more thorough checking by the team member. In addition, creating a greater sense of urgency for important assignments helps keep the team member from falling behind schedule.

Potential Complications

Make the team member's job easier by explaining any difficulties and problems that are likely to arise while doing the assignment. Your experience and knowledge of complications with related assignments can help prepare the team member for difficulties. Any techniques or tips you can give the team member for handling problems further improves the chances of a successfully completed assignment.

Discuss with the team member any helpful actions he or she could take to diminish the possibility of complications. To avoid conflicts with others in the organization, indicate to the team member anyone else who might have an interest in the results of the assignment. Of those interested people, indicate who should also be involved in the task. If problems are likely to interfere with the completion of an assignment, have the team member structure a plan for dealing with complications.

Results Orientation

Focus on the result to be achieved; don't try to delegate the method. Delegating the method puts unnecessary limitations on the person doing the task. Let the team member use her own knowledge and skills to come up with a way to get the job done. She might even find a better method than you thought possible!

Confirming Understanding

After the task has been communicated, get an acknowledgement from the team member that he understands and agrees to the assignment. If this step is omitted, you may find out later that the employee had objections. Perhaps the employee thought it was not the right thing to do or that the time allowed for completion was not realistic. In either case, you need to be certain any employee doubts, questions, or suggestions are expressed at the time you make the assignment.

Make sure the team member fully understands the task including its goals and priorities. Delegate what needs to be done as simply and directly as possible. Give precise instructions and anticipate the team member's questions.

It is often effective if you explain to the team member how you would do the assignment if it were yours to complete—especially if this is the first such assignment you've delegated to the employee. Be sure to remind the team member, however, that he can complete the assignment in whatever manner he deems most effective. Keep in mind that telling the team member how to complete an assignment is not a preferred long-term means of delegating work. Effective delegation encourages involvement and allows flexibility in completing an assignment. If you focus primarily on the results to be accomplished, rather than *how* the results are to be accomplished, team members will learn more, take more initiative, and have greater enthusiasm for completing the task.

As with any communication, you stand the chance of being misunderstood. Team members must know what is *not* being delegated. One way to diminish the possibility of completing the wrong task is to have the team member explain the assignment to you *after* you explain it to her. This lets you verify what the team member heard and what she considered important.

Another simple but important method for clarifying communication is to confirm the oral delegation in a written memo. It might be better still to have the team member confirm the discussion in writing. In this way, you can easily determine whether you were clearly understood, while at the same time delegating another task that a team member is capable of handling.

For routine assignments, it helps to have written policies that a team member can easily follow. Such policies make it easy for team members to make minor decisions on an assignment without having to contact the manager. Written policies also help ensure that there is consistency between similar tasks done by different people.

SETTING PERFORMANCE STANDARDS

Communicating the performance standards by which the team member will be evaluated ensures that the team member knows what good performance is. Performance standards help you and employees monitor performance and serve as a basis for evaluation. An indicator that performance standards are not being set is related in the following scenario:

> To determine whether an organization has clear performance standards, employees can be asked: "Are you doing a good job?" Most people will respond to this question by saying: "Yes, I think so." A revealing follow-up question would then be: "How do you know?" The typical response: "I haven't been criticized by my manager lately."[3]

Be able to measure and give feedback to team members during the performance of a task. Setting performance standards provides a mechanism for measurement and feedback. Performance standards include specifying different amounts of time, different degrees of quality, quantity, and cost. Effective managers communicate their expectations of performance without relying on the power of their position. Instead they use personal persuasion and leadership skills to emphasize what they expect of the team member. Effective managers make it clear that they have confidence in the team member's abilities to achieve superior performance.

FIGURE 4–2
Set Three Levels of Performance Standards

Outstanding = Completes assignments
early
Acceptable = Completes assignments
on time
Minimal   = Completes assignments

Guidelines for Setting Performance Standards

For successful delegation, you and the team member must agree on performance standards for the task. It's most effective if performance standards are determined for three levels of performance: minimal, acceptable, and outstanding. Several questions need to be clarified when setting performance standards.

Quality parameters. It is important for you and the team members to agree on standards of quality. What parameters of quality do you expect? Which parameters define exceptional, fair, and poor quality?

Amount of resources. Team members must know what boundaries they have to stay within while performing the task. How much time, money, or other resources can they use? What are the budgets for the task? What are the deadlines for the task?

Presentation of results. Team members need to understand what type of results you expect to see. Specify the form the results are to be presented in. Be as specific as possible about your expectations. It helps to give team members samples of the type of results you expect.

Guidelines for Setting Performance Measures

Central to setting performance standards is determining measures of performance. Performance measurements can be made through observations, surveys, interviews, and analyses of reports and records. The following guidelines are useful for determining performance measurements.

Simple. Measurements should be simple and easy for team members to understand.

Reliable. Measurements should be reliable. A measure is reliable if an increase in the measurement indicates an increase in performance. For example, the number of phone calls made does not necessarily measure the number of sales closed.

Unbiased. Measurements should be fair and unbiased. Measurements are unfair or biased when those collecting the information have a vested interest in the outcome or when the measure involves too much subjectivity. If the outcomes are observable and verifiable by anyone who examines the results, then the measures are fair and unbiased.

Organized. Measurements should be organized so they reflect the performance of the smallest work unit. This allows you to detect problem areas quickly and effectively.

Stable. Measurements should be stable and not subject to outside influences and contingencies. If too many uncontrollable variables can affect the measurement, the measurement is not stable.[4]

PROVIDING AUTHORITY

Assigning a task without granting the appropriate level of authority makes it unlikely the task can be accomplished. The team member lacks the power to obtain and use necessary resources. For example, if a team member can't request help from support staff, he or she may be unable to complete the task on time. If the team member is denied access to records, he or she may be unable to complete the task at all.

Any delegated task must have with it a delegated level of authority. No delegation takes place if a team member is not granted authority to complete his responsibility. Delegating authority gives a team member latitude to spend money, direct or seek assistance from others, or represent the department or the company. The level of authority granted to the team member has a drastic effect on the alternatives that the team member considers.

If you give the team member too little authority, she can't handle the assignment effectively or is limited to the method you dictate for implementation. If you grant too much authority, you might feel uneasy about the team member making a mistake and costing the department extra money or time.

Give all assignments a commensurate level of authority. You grant authority to enable independent action and decision making for the period in which the task is being completed. This authority can be defined as the permission to act with the power of the delegator, as your surrogate.

Mistakes in Granting Authority

Managers make several common mistakes when granting authority.[5]

Commensurate authority. Typically, a team member is not given enough authority to effectively complete the task. A labor relations manager served as chief negotiator for his company in collective bargaining sessions. He was given full authority to meet with the union and receive and discuss demands. However, he was required to call headquarters before making any nonroutine concessions. Most labor contract negotiations come to a point where the contract can be settled immediately. However, this negotiator did not have the authority to settle on the spot.

Ratification. Ratification means that the manager gives the team member after-the-fact approval of an action. So the team member proceeds at his own risk, and only finds out later—too much later—if the manager approves. Although at first glance such a policy appears to give the team member maximum control, the manager is really shirking responsibility. This policy is commonly used by managers who don't want to share authority with team members.

Accountability but not authority. Many managers want help with the work and responsibility but aren't willing to share the power, influence, and status that accompany authority. Granting accountability without the appropriate level of authority leads to frustration and unsatisfactory results.

Authority survives the action. A manager must grant authority before the task and support it after the task. For example, a president delegates to a vice president the task of replacing incompetent department heads. The vice president decides to remove a particular department head. After the decision is made, the president intervenes, persuading the manager (using his power and position) to back down. The vice president becomes convinced that she has no authority to implement her own decisions.

Authority is personal. Authority needs to be based on personal differences such as accountability, competence, and circumstances surrounding the delegation.

Levels of Authority

Don't be afraid to place someone out on a limb. If you're unsure about the risks involved, however, ease the person into the activity gradually by giving only the appropriate level of authority for action. The following defines four different levels of authority that can be granted when delegating a task.

Level A, no authority. If the assignment is especially important or difficult, or if the team member is new or working on a new type of assignment, assume all authority yourself. The following characteristics define this level of authority:

- You determine the team member's responsibilities.
- You set the team member's goals, develop project plans, and set performance standards for the completion of the task.
- You effectively communicate the responsibilities, goals, performance standards, and project plans to the team member.

- The team member consults regularly with you to inform you of progress made.
- The team member consults you on all problems encountered.

This level of authority should be used as infrequently as possible, however, since it indicates a low level of trust. Even so, it is appropriate when you have doubts about the successful completion of a task or when the task is so important that you want a high degree of involvement.

Level B, minimal authority. As the team member gains experience, allow her greater latitude in action. The following characteristics define this level of authority:

- You determine the team member's responsibilities.
- You, together with the team member, set the team member's goals, develop project plans, and set performance standards for the completion of the task.
- The team member consults regularly with you to inform you of progress made.
- The team member consults you on difficult problems.

This method allows team members a say in determining their goals and performance standards, keeps you informed of the team members' progress, and gives you an opportunity to intervene if difficult problems arise.

Level C, medium authority. This level of authority allows the team member to make some levels of decisions without you. Characteristics of this level include:

- You determine the team member's responsibilities.
- The team member sets her own goals, develops project plans, and sets performance standards for the completion of the task.

- The team member gets your approval on the goals, plans, and performance standards before acting on them.
- The team member consults regularly with you to inform you of progress made.
- The team member consults you on difficult problems only if the team member thinks it's necessary.

For this level of authority, the team member is delegated a task such as "handling customer complaints." The team member sets up the goals, plans, and performance standards for accomplishing this responsibility. The team member then acts autonomously (with regular status reports to you) and consults you only if she encounters a difficult problem or customer.

Level D, complete authority. When the team member is a trusted employee with demonstrated competence in the type of task assigned, you can grant complete authority. You are completely removed from the assignment, even after it is completed. This is the level you should hope to achieve with most team members on most assignments. When properly executed, this level gives you more discretionary time and the confidence that the work is being completed as scheduled.

Characteristics of this level of authority include:

- You along with the team member determine the team member's responsibilities.
- The team member sets the team member's goals, develops project plans, and sets performance standards for the completion of the task.
- The team member acts on the goals, plans, and performance standards; the only consultation with you is a regular status report.

FIGURE 4–3
Characteristics of Four Levels of Authority

	Level A	Level B	Level C	Level D
Determines Responsibilities	Manager	Manager	Manager	Manager and Team Member
Sets Goals, Plans, Standards	Manager	Manager and Team Member	Team Member	Team Member
Gets Approval on Goals, Plans, Standards	—	—	Yes	No
Submits Periodic Progress Reports to Manager	Yes	Yes	Yes	Yes
Consults Manager on All Problems	Yes	No	No	No
Consults Manager on Difficult Problems	Yes	Yes	If team member desires	No

With this level of authority, you have minimal interaction with the team member. The only interaction with the team member is a regular status report on how the team member is meeting his goals and performance standards. Figure 4–3 summarizes the characteristics of the four levels of authority.

LEVEL OF SUPPORT

Support from you and other support staff is a key element that needs to be well planned and communicated. The team member must know what resources are available to her, what you've done to prepare others to support the team member's role, and your availability for assistance.

Available Resources

It is important to discuss the issues that can help get the team member started on the task, as well as answer any initial questions that he might have about the assignment and the available resources. Who can directly assist the person with the task? Who can provide indirect help, perhaps by referring the team member to other resources? What information and resources are available for additional assistance? What types of problems can the team member bring to you? When will you be available to help with problems?

Notice to Others

With large or important assignments, help the team member by contacting key individuals the team member needs to work with and informing them of the team member's role. This will help establish the team member's credibility later when she contacts the individuals for the first time. It also gives everyone involved a clear understanding of their respective roles.

Availability of the Manager

The support you provide after an assignment is made is perhaps most important of all. Team members can tell when you are sincere in wanting to assist. Your level of support determines the importance the team member attaches to the task. It affects the amount of effort he is willing to put into the assignment. Be sure the team member knows what role you plan to take in completing the assignment.

Clearly explain each other's role in the task. This will help to make future interactions on the topic beneficial to the team member without allowing the team member to become dependent on you.

- What information will you provide or issues will you check on that the team member cannot do himself?
- What assistance are you most capable of providing the team member?
- Keep all promises you make to your team member.
- When should the team member contact you and about which matters?
- Encourage the team member to develop alternatives for action rather than simply bringing problems to you when they arise and requesting a solution.

OBLIGATION AND COMMITMENT

After you are certain the team member understands the assignment, be sure he agrees to do it. A sense of responsibility for completing the delegated task must be created and must be derived from the team member. The individual must agree to the assignment either routinely, by coercion, or by other means. Delegation is not complete until the individual commits to performing the assignment.

Assigning a task without creating a sense of obligation or responsibility is rarely successful. Don't leave an assignment with a team member unless you get a commitment for completion of the task by an agreed-on date. This is especially important for a sizable project that will last over an extended period of time. Keep alert for indications—either in statements or behavior—that the team member's sense of responsibility is weak.

The employee must have a sense of commitment and accountability for the task. As one of the resources at her disposal, make yourself available to assist with the task. Make clear, however, that the assignment belongs to the employee and she must resolve any problems that arise. Although it's difficult to delegate a task you know you can do well, fight the tendency and force the team member to fulfill her obligation.

ESTABLISHING REWARDS

Be sure to notice the team member's performance and apply consequences. If you fail to establish a reward, team members will initially try harder to receive some kind of recognition. If recognition is never forthcoming, they will decide that good performance makes no difference. If you don't treat good performers differently there is no motivation for others to become good performers.

Tell the team member in advance the positive and negative consequences to expect for excellent and poor performance. Hersey and Blanchard state that there are four types of consequences that make a difference when working with team members: praise, redirection, renegotiation of goal and/or standards, and reprimand.[6]

Praise

Praise is one of the most important aspects of a reward system. Praise means showing sincere appreciation to the team member for a job well done. Praise needs to follow the accomplishment of a goal or the successful completion of a milestone.

Redirection

Use redirection when you determine that the team member didn't understand the original delegation. Return to the beginning of the delegation and restate with greater clarity the goals and a revised plan for reaching those goals.

Renegotiation

If a performance standard ends up being too low or too high, renegotiate the delegation. List and explain the new responsibilities for the renegotiated task and the new set of performance measurements and standards.

Reprimand

A reprimand states your displeasure with the team member's performance. Use reprimands for instances of poor performances or when a person with demonstrated ability should be doing better. Don't reprimand new team members learning a new job until you gather all the facts.

SUMMARY

Effective delegation is more than simply telling a team member to perform a task. The delegation process is a mutual consultation and agreement between you and your team members. There are five important steps you must take when delegating a task to a team member: (1) clearly communicate what the team member is responsible for, (2) communicate the performance standards by which the team member will be evaluated, (3) make sure the team member has enough authority to complete the task, (4) establish the mechanisms for communication and control, and (5) establish a reward system. Completing all of these steps ensures that team members understand what they are supposed to be doing and that they will be held accountable for the task.

Communicating the responsibilities of a task to a team member includes setting the goals of the task, making sure the team member clearly understands the goals of the task, explaining the relative importance of the task, and describing the potential complications that the team member might run into. Setting performance standards for a task includes developing and clearly communicating the performance measures for the task. You must delegate the appropriate level of authority for a task. Delegating the appropriate level of authority includes determining how much the team member will be involved in the planning process and how much you will be monitoring the progress of the task. Establishing the communication and control system specifies how you will monitor the team member's progress. Establishing a reward system specifies the consequences of good and bad performance.

Chapter Five

Monitoring Delegation

Barry, a bank executive, found that even the best effort in delegating can fall short if progress isn't adequately monitored. Barry delegated an assignment to John and later found that John hesitated to ask for help when he was having difficulty. Barry and John set up goals and performance standards for the task, but their system for monitoring was ineffective. On his weekly activity reports, John never indicated that there were problems. Yet John couldn't finish the project on time because he was having trouble obtaining necessary information from other departments.

John didn't want to mention the problem to Barry because he thought Barry would think he was incapable. Just before the project was due, Barry found out it would be late. "Why didn't you let me know sooner that you were having trouble?" Barry asked John. "I thought I could work it out myself, and I didn't want to bother you with another problem," John explained.

Problems such as John's are exactly what a manager's job is all about. Barry could have suggested several ways to obtain the needed information including the right people to contact. He could have helped strategize the best approach and perhaps even role-played the situation with John. Alternatively, he could have changed the assignment, making the information unnecessary, at least for the time being.

You might think John made a mistake keeping silent, but Barry failed as well. Barry failed to come to an

understanding with John about how to handle difficulties. Controlling and monitoring a delegated activity is an
important skill every manager needs to know. It is one of
the prime responsibilities of managers at all levels. Progress has to be monitored by establishing a feedback
system for current, accurate information.

WHY MONITOR DELEGATION?

Monitoring helps you catch problems as they arise, and it
also helps motivate team members toward successful
completion of a task. Team members must understand the
consequences of their performance. Monitoring includes:

- Determining how well team members are meeting
  agreed-on performance standards.
- Communicating to team members how well they
  are meeting performance standards.

Paul Hersey and Ken Blanchard summarize the importance of monitoring performance:

> The only consequence that tends to increase the frequency of
> behavior is a positive consequence. And yet, the two most
> frequent responses people consistently get to their perfor-
> mance are negative responses and no responses. This leads
> to the "leave alone/zap" style of management. . . .[1]

Controls help you measure and communicate to team
members whether desired performance standards are
being obtained. Controls provide a means of measuring
and analyzing team members' actions at established
checkpoints. Controls enforce accountability. Without
controls, you have no way of knowing if and when an assignment will be completed and how well it will be done.
An effective control system is beneficial for the following
reasons.

Problem Identification

Controls, when properly implemented, help you identify problems and deviations as they arise. By comparing actual results to established standards, you can see areas of existing and potential problems.

Good controls help you catch problems before they become too large and either delay or obstruct the completion of the assignment. Deviations can be identified in enough time to be corrected, so the employee can still meet the deadline.

Motivation

Controls are a motivator for achieving more and better work. Recent studies indicate a significant increase in production when team members are given an increased amount of feedback about their performance. This feedback helps to fine-tune their performance.

To be most effective at both tracking and encouraging performance, monitoring needs to be specific, individually tailored, and focused on factors that an individual can control. The control system anticipates problems before they become major obstacles. It also serves as a stimulant for corrective actions to those problems.

TIGHT VERSUS LOOSE CONTROL

One of the fundamental choices in monitoring delegated activities is the degree of control you impose. With tight control, you examine each step of the assignment in detail. This is appropriate for inexperienced employees or when you want to compensate for a team member's deficiencies. With tight control, there is less chance for confusion about the assignment itself or the team member's authority. Tight control is most efficient in environments that change infrequently and where the role of the team member remains stable. Tight controls are also appropriate for especially important assignments or in crisis situations.

Loose control allows team members greater freedom in implementing an assignment. They assume responsibility not only for completing the assignment, but for informing you when there are unexpected developments or problems. The team member may also be responsible for notifying you when the assignment is complete.

Loose control is the preferred method when dealing with professionals. It allows maximum use of each team member's initiative, ingenuity, and imagination. It also increases team member self-development and decreases the amount of your time needed. Loose control is best achieved by gradually allowing team members greater freedom as they demonstrate skill in effectively completing assignments.

The appropriate level of control depends on the task involved and the desired results. If the team member is inexperienced, if the assignment is difficult or vague, of if accuracy and timing are important, consider using tighter controls. If the employee is trusted and able, experienced with such tasks, and motivated to perform well, or the activity is less important, consider using looser controls.

Variables Affecting Control

Be sure to clarify the means of monitoring and obtaining feedback with your team member. The extent to which monitoring is used and relied on, however, will vary greatly with different employees. The experience of the team member, the length of time he or she has been working for you, and the importance of the assignment affect the degree of control you select.

Team member experience. A team member who is an expert in the area of an assignment obviously requires less guidance. Likewise, if she has done a similar task before, you need to spend minimal time monitoring her work.

Team member motivation. A highly motivated team member has high energy for taking on new tasks and assignments. This makes the assignment easier to do and typically easier to monitor. The individual can be directed toward aspects of the assignment that need special attention. The person is likely to be a quick learner and eager to accept more responsibility.

Working relationship. If you know a team member well and have been working with him for several years, you'll need to do less monitoring than you do with a new hire. In any working group, people develop their own communication style, which helps them create a strong, effective relationship. In such relationships, trust is high. The individuals know each other's style, moods, and subtle ways of communicating. Assignments may need to be less clearly explained, and you can be assured that problems will be brought to your attention.

Task importance. If a task is important to you, your control system should reflect that fact. Monitoring should be more frequent and more detailed. Unless trust is especially high, make sure you follow the progress of the assignment closely.

CHARACTERISTICS OF EFFECTIVE CONTROL SYSTEMS

An effective control system tells you and your team member when progress is falling short of the target. Controls give everyone feedback about the progress made against established goals. Several factors are important in any control system:

Predetermined Standards

In order to determine acceptable performance, you need to establish guidelines to evaluate performance. As mentioned earlier, these guidelines or standards are best communicated to the team member at the time you assign a task.

Open Communication

Be sure employees can approach you whenever they experience difficulties or have doubts about being able to meet a deadline. Be available. Answer questions and give guidance, but don't tell the team member what to do or how to do it. Telling a team member what to do effectively rescinds the delegation.

Tailored Controls

Tailor your controls to the assignment. Pick the right warning indicators. For example, accounting data may be too general to provide useful information on how well a project is progressing.

Accurate Measurement

It may not suffice to simply ask an employee how an assignment is going. You may need to probe and seek specifics. For example, ask a team member who is responsible for payment collections to divide past-due accounts into categories (30 days past due, 30 to 60 days past due, etc.) and report on improvements made in each group. Initial

FIGURE 5–1
Feedback Is Fundamental to Good Delegation

objectives need to be stated in measurable terms or you won't be able to monitor progress.

Adequate Frequency

The monitoring system should allow you to evaluate progress systematically. Of course, frequency of monitoring is relative to the length and scope of the assignment. Casual discussion at the half-way point may suffice for a task that takes a week or two. Larger projects that extend over several months may need to be evaluated in depth every month. For some projects, you may need to review each stage and the contribution of each person involved. But avoid excessive monitoring where it isn't warranted.

Correction Capabilities

A control system falls short if it provides only feedback and doesn't allow for corrective action. If performance deviates from agreed-on standards, discuss the situation with the team member and decide on a plan for corrective action. If necessary, change the task, revoke the individual's authority, and/or assign the task to someone else.

Internally Consistent

If you use a different control system for different team members performing similar tasks, tell them why. One employee may be more experienced and need less monitoring. But if you fail to explain, you may appear to be acting inconsistently or giving someone preferential treatment.

MEANS OF MONITORING DELEGATION

There are a variety of techniques for monitoring delegation including assignment logs, personal follow-up, sampling techniques, progress reports, management by exception, statistical controls, and historical comparison.

Assignment Log

A first step to monitoring assignments is developing a well-organized assignment log. You and your work group need some type of system for tracking what tasks are assigned, to whom, and when they are to be completed. Some managers simply list assigned projects in the left-hand margin of a page and place headings across the top: "Assigned to," "When Assigned," "When Due," "Complications," and "Comments." Then they review and update the page regularly. But remember: if you can't measure what you want, you won't get it!

Another system involves keeping a folder on each team member with a page for each assignment. For many assignments, the page would be a memo summarizing and confirming actions the team member will be taking. Such a file makes it easier for you to systematically discuss the progress of all the employee's projects. You can add notes to the assignment sheets as problems and changes arise and discard the sheets when the project is completed.

Personal Follow-Up

Studies show that, when monitoring is needed, informal methods are the most effective. It is much more effective to informally ask a team member how a specific task is coming along rather than hear about it in a formal report. Most team members soften negative information in a formal communication. If you rely solely on formal communications, you may be surprised and disappointed when the final deadline is missed.

A team member knows that an assignment you ask about frequently is more important than one you mention once and never monitor. But your interest must be sincere to be effective. Ask specific questions about the assignment. Such questions not only indicate your interest, they help you examine the progress of an assignment more closely. Although personal monitoring is time consuming, the fact that you take the time tells the team member that completion is important to you. You don't have to spend a great deal of time in follow-up, but it does need to be quality time that is both focused and sincere.

FIGURE 5–2
*Personal, Informal Follow-Up Indicates High Managerial
Interest and Task Importance*

Personal reports can be done through face-to-face meetings or updates on voice-mail or electronic mail. However, don't overreact to bad news if you want to continue
to be informed.

Sampling Techniques

Depending upon the type of work being completed, one
technique of monitoring performance quality is by sampling. Take a representative sample of the team member's
work to establish the quality of the entire project or area

of responsibility. For example, you can visit a production area or attend a meeting in which the team member is giving a presentation.

Progress Reports

Progress or activity reports are useful as a secondary method of tracking delegated tasks. They provide another way for the team member to communicate problems and next steps. And, because activity reports summarize an employee's activity, they're useful references for performance reviews. Activity reports are effective as a supplemental means of monitoring activities, but don't rely on them exclusively for feedback. Employees rarely include negative information if they report problems at all. If a significant problem arises, it's better to hear about it in person as soon as possible rather than through a written report.

Management by Exception

Management by exception is based on the idea that controls are necessary only when there is a deviation from previously established standards. In essence, rather than being kept fully informed of an assignment's progress, you are told only of unexpected or unusual developments. This way you can control an operation with a minimum amount of effort. You focus on helping team members resolve unacceptable problems rather than trying to monitor all assignments all the time. However, don't use management by exception if problems are difficult to identify and any single error could cause significant damage.

David Sculley, senior vice president at Heinz who oversees the Weight Watchers line, provides an example of this technique: "We manage by exception generally"—

using variances from projections to provide clues that
something is going awry. "There's a goal post that is clear
for every manager in the company—yearly and quarterly.
Responsible managers won't make decisions inconsistent
with those goals. And secrets are not well kept in our
company. When we see a problem develop, we jump on
it!"[2]

Statistical Controls

Statistical control reports present data comparing your
operations with those of similar areas in your organization or industry. You can then evaluate how team members are doing based on indicators from the report. If
necessary, new control standards can be implemented or
changed to allow for a more efficient operation. Of course,
this method isn't beneficial for monitoring a specific task
or a team member in a unique situation.

Historical Comparison

Similar to statistical controls, a historical comparison focuses on the past performance of your area. Data is often
presented graphically to depict the rise and fall of production, for example, and the effectiveness of various
controls on monitoring past and current performance.
Historical trends help you see cycles in past performance
and forecast levels of desired performance.

Monitoring Delegation Using the PRICE System

Hersey's and Blanchard's PRICE (Pinpoint, Record, Involve, Evaluate) system is an effective model for establishing controls to monitor performance. The elements of
the PRICE system include the following.

Pinpoint. When delegating a task, pinpointing refers to identifying and communicating the responsibilities of the task to the team member. Methods for pinpointing, discussed in the previous chapter, include identifying key responsibilities of the team member, prioritizing those areas, and communicating what you expect. This objective is equally important for all levels of delegation.

Record. Once key responsibilities are identified and communicated, the next step is to record present performance in related areas. Recording current performance on related tasks provides a baseline of information from which to measure performance on the delegated task. Performance recording must be done systematically. Continue tracking information through the point where the team member is evaluated. It's important to prominently display or communicate the tracking. Graphically depicting progress in a prominent place can greatly improve a team member's performance. The amount of information you record depends on the level of delegation—less for a team member who is to act autonomously, more for someone who needs more interaction with you.

Involve. Involving team members in the task includes: (*a*) setting observable, measurable goals for the team members, (*b*) determining what kind of supervision and support the employees need (that is, the level of delegation), and (*c*) making sure team members know how they will be evaluated and what their rewards will be for successful completion. Methods for helping a team member become involved in a task were discussed in the previous chapter. The number and type of goals you set depend on the level of delegation.

Coach. Coaching includes (*a*) praising progress, (*b*) reprimanding or redirecting undesired performance,

FIGURE 5–3
The PRICE System Pays Off!

Pinpoint
Record
Involve
Coach
Evaluate

and (c) catching team members doing things right. No
matter what the level of delegation, coaching is always
important! Some managers monitor employees' performance but fail to give them feedback on their efforts until
they make a mistake. Coaching requires constant communication with team members.

Evaluate. Evaluating team members' performance includes (a) letting team members know how
they're doing, (b) promoting their self-confidence, and
(c) determining future strategies for performance improvement. At predetermined and periodic intervals, sit
down with the team member and evaluate her performance. Review all the interaction between you and the
employee and assess her progress toward the goal. Remember, you retain ultimate responsibility for the delegated task. Take responsibility to make sure team
members successfully complete it. During evaluation,
assess your own leadership behavior. If you requested a
change, did you emphasize and reinforce it? Did you use
consequences effectively? Did you allow enough time for

the desired performance to occur? Could you handle un-expected problems better in the future?[3]

COMMON PROBLEMS WITH CONTROL SYSTEMS

Several problems occur with control systems including reverse delegation, default decision making, wrong pur-pose, wrong person, not accurate, and biased controls.

Reverse Delegation

Reverse delegation occurs when a team member turns an assignment around so the manager ends up doing it. For example, the team member may ask the manager a question for which the manager doesn't know the answer. The manager then agrees to find the answer although the team member could do so just as easily.

"Delegating upward," as reverse delegation is also known, can be avoided if you clearly define whose problem is whose before agreeing to help. If the matter is the team member's responsibility, make suggestions about what the team member could do. Don't spend time on the delegated activity in the absence of the team member. The team member's job is to help you with your needs; your job is to train the team member to help.

Default Decision Making

Default decision making occurs when the team member tries to minimize risk by having the manager make all the decisions and choices. Not only is the team member robbed of valuable experience, but you are no longer managing. Force team members to make their own decisions!

Wrong Purpose

Many controls are set up to catch mistakes rather than prevent them. For example, if a team member is tracking expenditures, set up a system to flag excessive or disproportionate spending instead of one that merely indicates when you've exceeded the total budget. Such reports may need to be augmented with information tailored to the specific assignment.

Wrong Person

Control systems should be designed to provide feedback to the team member, as well as the manager. You can use the information to decide if corrective action is needed.

Not Accurate

A feedback or control system that can be manipulated or that doesn't provide enough information is ineffective. The control system should not only inform you about problems, but also where the problems are and why they are happening. Controls should be specific enough to give you insight into problems. Don't rely on standard reports as the only source of feedback.

Biased Controls

Controls should represent not only costs, for example, but also the returns on those costs. A project may go over budget, but the extra costs may be justifiable if a change was requested by top management or a customer. In this case, a strictly enforced cost control system may undermine the goal.

TAKING CORRECTIVE ACTION

Be sure to give team members an adequate chance to do the work without interference. Nothing undermines confidence more than having a manager intervene and tell team members what to do. Depending on the amount of control established, make allowance for errors and give team members time to correct them. Don't overreact to problems. Encourage negative information so you and the team member can discuss and learn from it. If you react too strongly, team members won't tell you what you need to know.

If progress veers too far from planned or allowable guidelines, take corrective action. This action may consist of any or all of the following steps depending upon the severity of the deviation: discussion and warning, rescinding authority, and/or reassigning the task.

Discussion and Warning

When you first have doubts about an assignment being completed on time, raise those doubts to the team member. Don't delay in the hope that the situation will improve. Once problems occur, the situation is likely to deteriorate further. Discuss your concerns with the team member and agree on a plan for ensuring that the assignment quickly gets back on target. If the situation doesn't improve, conduct another meeting with the team member. At the second meeting, warn the team member that further intervention will be necessary if adequate progress isn't made.

Rescinding Authority

Any delegation of authority is granted on a temporary basis and is rescindable. Keep this fact in mind when a team member is not performing as expected. Authority may also be rescinded when there are organizational changes such as altered objectives, reorganizations, or new policies. Then you can grant authority to other individuals or give it back to the same person, whatever you deem appropriate. Remember that relationships develop through interaction. Every time you rescind authority, you weaken your working relationship with your employee and make future interactions more difficult.

Reassigning Activities

When you face the prospect of a project or assignment not being completed on schedule, consider reassigning the work. You can reassign the project to a more experienced team member or divide it among several employees. You can let the team member retain a portion of the original assignment, but monitor the person more closely.

SUMMARY

Effective delegation requires the establishment of control systems to monitor progress. How much control and monitoring you use depends on several variables including team member experience, team member motivation, the working relationship between you and the team member, and the importance of the assignment. Effective control systems motivate team members and allow you to identify and rectify problems before they get out of hand. Characteristics of effective control systems include performance standards, open communication, tailored controls, adequate frequency of monitoring, correction capabilities, and internal consistency. A manager can implement control systems using techniques such as personal follow-up, progress reports, regular status meetings, or sampling techniques. Be sure to praise employees for good performance and take corrective action when necessary.

Chapter Six

Evaluating Delegation

One dimension of effective delegation that Jim hoped to improve on was the evaluation of delegated tasks. He often made the mistake of not giving enough feedback to team members after assignments were completed. Consequently, many of his team members repeated the same mistakes. Some didn't know better because Jim never spoke with them about the mistakes or offered suggestions for improvement. Others repeated mistakes because Jim didn't seem to mind—at least he never said anything about them! Jim often corrected mistakes himself. He didn't want to seem critical of team members' work, and he rarely complained about the errors they made. Jim's attitude about evaluating assignments not only cost him precious time, but it also created bad habits among his team members.

As a follow-up to any assignment, appraise the completed task and discuss your evaluation with the team member. Measure the degree of success against the standards you agreed on when you initially made the assignment. The evaluation stage should provide insight for both you and the team member, showing how well each of you performed your respective role. This stage should also provide a measure of how well you worked together.

In evaluating the delegated tasks, answer the following questions:

- Was the delegated task completed as intended in a timely manner?
- What could you do to better delegate such a task in the future?

COMPARING RESULTS WITH INITIAL GOALS

The better an assignment was delegated, the easier it is to determine if desired results were obtained. Was the delegated activity completed as requested? Was it completed on time? The most effective approach to evaluation measures the team member's accomplishments or results against the intended objectives. When results aren't achieved, usually team members misunderstood the assignment or lacked the authority to complete it.

Pay special attention to these areas when delegating a task. Make certain your communication is clear. Tell team members to let you know if the authority you granted is inadequate. Evaluate the team member's role and your own.

EVALUATING THE TEAM MEMBER'S ROLE

The employee who accepts responsibility for doing a task carries the burden of seeing that the task is completed as promised. The most effective way to evaluate a team member is by comparing results with objectives. Actual results should determine if the team member succeeded. Don't let personality factors cloud your judgment. Evaluation must be objective.

Once quantitative aspects are determined—whether results were achieved as specified—you can assess other aspects of the team member's work. This closer look provides insight into other factors that may have affected results—including the employee's work style. Some additional factors to evaluate include the following.

Quality

What was the quality of the work done? When you evaluate the quality of a delegated task, concentrate on the quality of the *results*. Were results adequate to meet desired goals? Did the team member exceed expectations? Exert extra effort? Was attention given to details of the assignment?

Efficiency

Did the team member achieve the desired results efficiently? Did the team member spend an inordinate amount of time or use excessive resources?

Did the team member complete the assignment on time or ahead of schedule? Did she have and show a sense of urgency? Did she do the right things at the right time? Did she allocate her time effectively between different parts of the assignment? Did she bring problems or questions to your attention at the appropriate time?

Creativity

Was the team member resourceful and creative at overcoming obstacles? Did he seek the opinion of others about how to complete the task most effectively? Did he show insight and vision in completing the assignment?

Cooperation

Did the team member achieve results while strengthening relationships with others, both inside and outside of the department? Was he successful at obtaining the cooperation of support staff, peers, and other managers? Did he demonstrate effective interpersonal skills and sensitivity in working with others?

DISCUSSING THE MANAGER'S EVALUATION

An important part of evaluating any delegated activity is to discuss the evaluation with the team member. Of course, it may not be practical to hold such discussions after every assignment, but it's important to do so after major assignments. (Discuss more routine responsibilities with the employee at her scheduled performance reviews.) The evaluation should be a two-way exchange of perceptions and feedback on each other's work style, and insights (positive and negative) should be mutually explored.

Positive and Negative Feedback

A good evaluation always includes both positive and negative information, even though such an approach is counter to human nature. Managers often try to avoid criticizing team members. They either fail to comment on a team member's performance or make brief, positive statements regardless of whether the assignment was satisfactorily completed.

Begin each evaluation with positive statements about what you liked and why. This helps to set a positive, constructive tone for the review discussion. Include any unexpected positive surprises about the person's work on the assignment. Then move on to explain any negative evaluation.

Both positive and negative comments are needed for team members to understand what they are doing well and where they need to improve their performance. If you withhold negative comments, a team member won't recognize problem areas and will continue to make similar mistakes. This isn't fair to the team member. And the manager is shirking his responsibility because he is uncomfortable in giving negative feedback. Give team members the advantage of a *complete* evaluation.

Giving Constructive Criticism

There is a skill in giving negative information in a way that will be constructively received and used to the team member's best advantage. Be sincere in wanting to help the team member improve. Offer suggestions for improvement along with your criticism.

Don't overemphasize mistakes; keep errors in relation to your overall satisfaction with the results.

Constructive criticism highlights solutions and better approaches for future assignments. Focus on job-related issues that the employee can change or control. Don't bring up personality traits over which the team member may have little control. Use specifics in the discussion, and avoid broad general comments that are apt to have less meaning. Use comments that are future-oriented, not past-oriented. Of course, all reviews should be held private.

The Value of Making Mistakes

Accept the fact that employees will make mistakes whenever they are given responsibility for new activities. The way you handle those mistakes makes a major difference in whether the individual is willing to take risks and attempt new tasks in the future. If a person never falls down when learning to ski, for example, chances are she will never get to be a better skier. Likewise, if you chastise an employee for a mistake, that person will be less likely to take initiative again.

Even if the activity was not completed satisfactorily, everyone should learn something from the outcome. Ask the team member what he learned from the experience and what he would do differently next time. Ask for suggestions that could improve the work environment and seek comments on how you could work better with the employee in the future.

If you discuss mistakes, emphasize what could have been done to prevent them and what the individual can do next time to avoid similar mistakes. This approach doesn't stifle initiative. As the person gains experience, mistakes naturally diminish, and with the proper encouragement, they will.

EVALUATING THE MANAGER'S ROLE

The manager's role is often overlooked in the evaluation of assignments. Whatever the team members achieve or don't achieve reflects on the skills and abilities of the manager. If you fail to provide a conducive atmosphere, you may be equally at fault for the team member's mistakes and shortcomings.

One of the most prevalent mistakes managers make is failure to delegate enough authority. Other items managers should assess to evaluate if they are delegating effectively include involvement, communication, agreement, follow through, and accountability.

Involvement

Were team members given the opportunity to be involved in the assignment early in the delegation process? Were they allowed to participate in decisions that affect their assignments and responsibilities? Were they given room and encouraged to immerse themselves in projects? Did team members seek additional responsibility? Did you take an active interest in assignments after they were delegated? At minimum, you must stay involved enough to monitor the agreed-on performance standards.

Communication

Was the assignment clearly understood? Did you verify that the team member clearly understood the assignment? Did the team member communicate his or her ideas and plans? Did you establish methods for ongoing communication? Were you accessible to team members when they need to consult you? Did you communicate frequently about the assignment's progress?

Agreement

Did the team members agree with your expectations and with the schedule? Did they agree on the manner and frequency of their performance evaluations?

Follow Through

Did you and your team members follow through on completing activities as promised? Did you support team members when they needed it? Did you find out from each team member what he or she could do to help others do a better job?

Accountability

Did you clearly explain the team member's accountability and make sure she understood? Did you assign accountability for each delegated responsibility? Did you hold team members accountable after the assignment was completed? Did you evaluate them and give both positive and negative feedback?

Throughout the delegation process, ask yourself if you are delegating in the best way possible. Are you delegating everything you could? How can you improve? What tasks do you spend time on that could be effectively handled by team members? If you were unable to work for the next one to six months, would your area still operate smoothly?

REWARDING EXCEPTIONAL PERFORMANCE

If you want exceptional performance from a team member to continue, recognize and reward it. Otherwise, team members won't know that you're aware of their performance or care about the quality of their work. Reinforcement of exceptional performance is a simple, fundamental rule of management, yet many managers ignore it. Remember: you get what you reward!

Failure to reinforce desired behavior undermines effectiveness. It can create major obstacles to accomplishing the goals of the department. Your best people will leave the organization, the next-best people will become mediocre, and those you hoped would leave will become permanent fixtures. Reward exceptional performance with exceptional salary increases, promote individuals who consistently perform well, and frequently thank everyone whose efforts you appreciate.

HOLDING TEAM MEMBERS ACCOUNTABLE

Identifying and responding to poor performance is as important as rewarding outstanding performance. If individuals aren't held accountable for poor performance, their poor performance will continue! However, errors are occasions for objective analysis and further training, not just punishment and blame. "People shouldn't be afraid to make mistakes," says Phil Gamache, corporate quality assurance manager at Lifeline Systems, a manufacturer of personal response systems. "Change is an end in itself, and whether everything works the first time around is entirely irrelevant."[1]

Inaction Yields Inaction

Many managers shy away from holding team members accountable for failure. They find such situations unpleasant, they're busy, or they want to give the employee the benefit of the doubt. Failing to confront poor performance, however, causes more problems in the future. If team members aren't held accountable for current assignments, they have little incentive to complete future ones. Not only will you perpetuate poor performance, but you will find it increasingly difficult to obtain good performance from others because they see no consequences for poor performance.

Accountability makes allowances for some factors that hinder successful completion of a task. For example, a team member may not have been granted an adequate level of authority. With complete accountability, however, a team member is held responsible even if factors outside her control prevented completion of the task.

Using the Rule of Errors

When evaluating an assignment, many managers use a somewhat more casual method of determining accountability called the rule of errors. The rule of errors focuses on degrees of success. The rule states that the employee is not accountable for minor mistakes or errors as long as overall results were successful and the main objectives of the assignment were fulfilled. The person's accountability is limited to the major decisions and actions he made. This rule focuses everyone's attention on the most important aspects of an assignment. If employees know in advance you're primarily concerned with the overall goal and not minor errors, they won't be afraid to act. With this style of evaluation, the team member will more readily recover from occasional mistakes.

SUMMARY

Evaluating delegated tasks helps you and your team members learn from mistakes. Evaluating the delegated task includes comparing the results with the initial goals, evaluating the team member's role, evaluating your role, and discussing the evaluation with the team member. The evaluation should include both positive and negative feedback. Be sure to look for ways to improve your own delegation skills.

Chapter Seven

Common Mistakes in Delegation

There are several pitfalls you must avoid during the delegation process. For example, Timothy Firnstahl, owner of a multimillion dollar restaurant chain, describes four problems he encountered in learning to delegate effectively:

> The first and most obvious problem was watching someone mess up a task I could do easily in half the time. I had to learn to keep my mouth shut since interceding would frustrate my new subordinate—not to mention use up the time I wanted to save. Handing over my company—my baby—to others and standing by as they did things their own way sorely tested my faith in human kind.
>
> The second problem had to do with identity, specifically mine. Delegating means shifting from the role of specialist—be it in finance, marketing or whatever—to that of generalist. It means becoming a leader, and leaders don't have precise job definitions. I had to give up the particular skills for which I was known and the gratification that went with applying them.
>
> Third was the problem of competitiveness. As an entrepreneur I am extremely competitive, and I had to watch while others reached ability levels superior to my own. I could no longer enjoy being unrivaled at various jobs—cooking, tending bar, training new workers. Delegating means letting others become the experts and hence the best.
>
> Finally, there was the problem of learning a whole new job. Now I had to decide where the organization should go, secure agreement from subordinates, and keep the company

FIGURE 7–1
Delegation Requires Skill and Practice to Perfect!

Adequate Planning
Balance of Tasks
Appropriate Authority
Adequate Explanation
Accurate Amount of Work
Necessary Level of Structure
Patience in Closure
Correct Control and Monitoring
Timely Evaluation and Review
Unceasing Accountability
Systematic Reinforcement/Rewards

---

on track. Learning this new job meant leaving my comfort zone for the unknown. It meant learning the art of leadership.[1]

This chapter discusses the most common mistakes managers make when delegating—and how to avoid them. The mistakes are categorized in the same order as the steps of effective delegation discussed earlier: preparing, assigning, monitoring, and evaluating delegation. This way, the discussion of common problems will also serve as a review of the key steps for effective delegation.

PROBLEMS IN PREPARING FOR DELEGATION

Keep in mind that delegation begins with preparation. Some common mistakes managers make in the preparation stage of delegating include failure to plan prior to delegating, assigning only unappealing tasks to employees, or assigning overlapping work assignments.

Insufficient Planning

Many managers don't systematically plan what they are and aren't going to delegate. As a result, work may be divided incorrectly and done by the wrong person—often the manager herself. She may run out of time to find someone else, or she may not trust anyone else to do the job. Set aside time to delegate properly. This time will be returned as team members assume a greater number of activities that you were once doing yourself.

Delegating Only Unappealing Tasks

The manager who delegates only boring, trivial, or unappealing tasks, saving the most exciting or visible work for himself, is a poor manager. Team members quickly realize what the manager is doing and lose respect for him. Assignments should include both desirable and less desirable activities equitably divided among team members according to their abilities and interests.

Overlapping Work Assignments

Whether intentional or not, problems in delegation sometimes occur when two or more individuals in an organization are responsible for doing the same task. This usually means that work assignments are too general or that different jobs in the same area have overlapping responsibilities. It can be corrected by specifically outlining responsibilities or by getting those involved together to decide who will do what.

PROBLEMS IN IMPLEMENTING DELEGATION

Be aware of the pitfalls that can occur in the implementation or assignment stage of the delegation process—failing to delegate authority, delegating without adequate explanation, overly structuring an assignment, and delegating too much.

Failure to Delegate Authority

This problem is probably the most common and significant shortcoming of managers who fail to delegate properly. You must grant a team member enough authority to complete the assignment. Responsibility without authority is a common complaint of team members who can't complete an assignment.

Think through the activities the team member will need to do to complete an assignment. Be certain the individual has the resources to do the job. Check with the team member periodically to determine if you've given her too little or too much authority. Adjust the level of authority accordingly.

Delegating without Adequate Explanation

Many managers dump an assignment on team members assuming they have full knowledge of its context, potential problems, and requirements. Not only is this ineffective, it's also unfair to the team member. The team member might need more information to do the assignment properly. He may also lack the appropriate skills, abilities, or interests. This manner of assigning a task convinces employees that the job is unimportant and unlikely to teach them anything valuable. Dumped tasks appear to be undesirable ones, and team members won't bring any enthusiasm or effort to the project. Ask the team member if you've provided enough information after you make an assignment.

Overly Structuring an Assignment

Another mistake managers make is to overly structure an assignment so the individual has too little latitude to make decisions. Sometimes the manager describes a preferred method of doing the job, one that she used successfully. This practice robs the team members of any challenge and excitement. It also limits the quality of work he might otherwise do. Insisting that a team member do an assignment in a specific way makes the team member feel like a puppet, since the task could be done by many other people. The team member is likely to dread the task, learn little from it, and leave the job as soon as possible. Limiting initiative is not part of most managerial jobs and should be avoided when delegating assignments. Focus instead upon what needs to be done, not on how to do it.

Delegating Too Much

A few managers delegate too many tasks too quickly. Although this problem is more infrequent, it has serious repercussions. A manager can completely divorce herself from any work and have team members do everything. Excessive delegation is a particular problem if team members aren't capable of handling the workload.

The manager also abdicates her managerial responsibilities and loses touch with the group and its purpose. Eventually this type of manager has no idea what work is being performed in her own department.

PROBLEMS IN MONITORING DELEGATION

The potential problems a manager needs to avoid in monitoring delegated tasks include undercutting team member authority, exerting inappropriate control over a team member, and completing or redoing delegated tasks.

Undercutting Team Member Authority

More frustrating to the team member than not receiving adequate authority is the practice of receiving inadequate support for the authority granted. Some managers develop a reputation for reversing their opinions and withdrawing support when the team member encounters difficulty with someone else in the organization.

For example, if the team member needs certain data and is having a difficult time obtaining it from other managers, a weak manager criticizes the team member and claims that he doesn't need the information. A strong manager discusses the problem with the team member and helps him decide on another source or approach. If necessary, the manager intervenes and calls the reluctant manager. Make certain, however, that you first allow the team member a chance to handle a problem himself.

Exerting Too Little or Too Much Control

One of the delegation skills that comes with experience is knowing the degree of monitoring to provide. The degree of monitoring also depends on the task, the team member, and the demands of the situation. Don't just hope that all goes well after you assign a task, but don't check up constantly either. If you're at a loss with a specific person or assignment, discuss the issue of control when first assigning the task so you and your team member reach a mutual understanding.

Completing or Correcting Delegated Tasks

Few things are more frustrating to a team member than having a manager complete a delegated assignment herself. Some managers are so anxious to get the job done that they work on it too. Others redo the assignment after the team member completes it because they don't think it was done correctly or don't like what was done. When asked about the latter case, managers often report that it's easier to change the work themselves. They assume the team member didn't understand what to do or didn't care about doing a better job.

As frustrating to the team member as having a manager redo the assignment is having a manager make changes to the assignment after it's completed. Changes indicate the manager wanted the assignment done a specific way all along. For example, a manager wants to make a certain recommendation to upper management. He asks a team member to write a report on the topic without mentioning his preference. The manager then rejects the team member's report and asks that it be redone until the report eventually recommends what the manager originally wanted.

Doing or redoing a delegated assignment undermines trust and effectiveness in the manager–team member relationship. Even if a team member does make a significant error, the learning that takes place by evaluating errors with the manager is valuable for future assignments.

PROBLEMS IN EVALUATING DELEGATION

There are several common pitfalls during the evaluation stage of delegation: failure to conduct review discussions, failure to hold the employee accountable for poor performance, and failure to reward superior performance.

Not Conducting Review Discussions

Since they are so busy, many managers never take time to adequately review assignments. But reviewing past performance is an essential step for improving future performance. Reviews help clarify communication, perceptions, and expectations for both you and your team member.

Not Holding Team Members Accountable

Few managers like to give negative information to a team member. They avoid confronting an employee with questions about his performance in the hope that he will improve on the next assignment. Many managers avoid negative feedback by saying they are giving the employee the benefit of the doubt; i.e., perhaps the assignment was poorly delegated, miscommunicated, or unrealistic.

Failure to discuss poor performance is unfair to the employee and an evasion of your managerial responsibilities. The employee will repeat mistakes since he has no idea that a problem exists. The employee may also take advantage of the situation. If employees are never held accountable for scheduled duties, they learn that it's acceptable to ignore deadlines.

Not Rewarding Performance

Like any behaviors not systematically reinforced, quality performance and team member effort diminish or disappear if they aren't recognized and rewarded. Team members who aren't recognized and rewarded for good performance lose enthusiasm for the next assignment. And their managers have trouble motivating their employees and achieving maximum output from the work group. Give credit where it is due. Thank a team member for her effort and show that you notice high-quality work.

WARNING SIGNS OF POOR DELEGATION

Many delegation mistakes will never come to your attention unless your manager or team member brings them up. And either may be reluctant to discuss a delegation problem with you. Following are several warning signs of poor delegation you can use to determine if you have a problem.

Too Busy

If you are constantly busy with work, under constant pressure, usually miss deadlines, spend a large amount of time on routine activities or operational details, you clearly have a delegation problem.

Often Surprised

If your team members frequently misunderstand what you want done and do something other than what you intended, if they don't perform the assigned task at all or constantly miss deadlines, if they frequently do a poor job, you have a delegation problem.

Productivity Drops

If your area is producing less than it once did, if operations seem less efficient than they could be, if team members aren't motivated to perform well, you have a delegation problem.

Team Members Leave

If your department has high turnover because employees don't feel challenged, if employees aren't learning much or feel you're difficult to work for, you have a delegation problem.

Promotion Bypass

If you've been passed over for a promotion because you have difficulty handling your current responsibilities, if you're considered too valuable in your current position, or if there's no other person in the department trained to take your place, you have a delegation problem.

If you believe you're not delegating effectively, confirm your suspicions by asking your team members for feedback on your delegation skills. Then formulate a plan to improve.

SUMMARY

Being aware of the common mistakes of delegation can help you avoid them and clarify or identify problems when they crop up. Evaluate each of these common problems to determine if any apply to you.

EPILOGUE

We've discussed why delegation is important; how to plan, implement, monitor, and evaluate delegation; and how to delegate to employees with different levels of experience. You have all the knowledge you need to be a great delegator. Now practice the techniques discussed in this book. First, gain comfort using the new skills; second, make those skills a habit.

If you make an honest effort to practice good delegation skills, you'll soon reap the rewards of your efforts. You'll see—if you don't already—the power of delegation. You will achieve far more for yourself, your team members, and the organization as a whole. Workloads will be more manageable and promotions more frequent. Everyone will win.

Appendix

Practicing Delegation— A Case Study

Assume you are a recently promoted manager of software development in a high-tech corporation. As this story unfolds, you find yourself in a variety of situations that call for different delegation decisions. Alternative decisions are presented, and you are asked to reflect on how you would handle the situation.

The scenario presented in this chapter is relevant to anyone with a specialized position who is promoted to manager—including sales, marketing, and engineering professionals.

This scenario will help you analyze your delegation style, understand your strengths, and see some of the mistakes you might make. Take time to understand the environment, people, and circumstances presented. Place yourself in the position of the manager, and try to evaluate how you would decide between the alternatives. Remember:

- THE FIRST STEP TOWARDS BECOMING A
  GOOD DELEGATOR IS TO UNDERSTAND YOUR
  STRENGTHS AND WEAKNESSES!

BACKGROUND AND BRIEFING

This management position is new for you. Up until now, you primarily had technical responsibilities. You performed so well in the technical role, however, the president and vice president of the company wanted to reward you and wanted you to take on additional management responsibilities. You want the new management responsibilities, although you aren't comfortable with the position yet. As Manager of Software Development, you will be confronted with such basic delegation functions as:

- Deciding what to delegate to who,
- Delegating a task, and
- Monitoring a delegated task

You work for Circuit Scan, Inc., a high-tech start-up company. At least 80 percent of all start-up companies fail. You're committed to helping make Circuit Scan one of the 20 percent that succeeds!

Firm Description

Circuit Scan is a venture capital company developing a new product to scan circuit boards and detect construction errors in the boards (such as defective soldering of the chip joints. Circuit board inspection systems can be put in a manufacturing line to isolate defective boards before they get out in the field. Such inspection systems can be used by computer manufacturers, the auto industry, and the government, and they have various commercial applications. Many manufacturers currently invest a tremendous amount of human resources into manually and visually inspecting circuit boards for defects. You can imagine how difficult it is to look at circuit boards all day, boards that might have 100 chips on each side. Successful automated circuit board inspection systems offer tremendous cost savings to circuit board manufacturers.

Successful automated circuit board inspection is a very difficult problem, and vendors have had a tough time developing a cost-effective solution. The most successful systems take different pictures of the image from different angles and locations, digitize the pictures into a computer, and develop software to analyze the digitized images for defects.

Circuit Scan uses a promising new approach. Its inspection system produces a three-dimensional image of the circuit board, which provides more information than other companies' two-dimensional images. However, there are a lot of unknowns. And each system will cost $300,000 to $400,000.

Circuit Scan has an agreement with Computers Unlimited, a major computer company, to install an inspection system at one of Computers Unlimited's manufacturing sites. The system will be installed in one year as a beta test site. This is an important deadline. Computers Unlimited is Circuit Scan's first customer—and it may become a major one by purchasing 50 to 200 systems over the next few years. Continued funding from the venture capital companies depends on a successful beta test site.

Reader's Role

You are one of the four original founders of Circuit Scan. The president, vice president, technology-development manager, and you left previous jobs two years ago to start Circuit Scan. You took quite a risk; the company went for one year without funding. Now the company's 25 employees work for you.

You are ultimately responsible for all software developed for the inspection system. The software has three important requirements.

- Throughput. The faster the software works, the higher the throughput of the system.
  Manufacturers need to achieve a minimum level of throughput for their manufacturing lines. Even

though an automated inspection system represents cost savings and an increase in quality, the inspection system can't be a bottleneck for the manufacturing line.

- Accuracy. The software must achieve a certain level of accuracy in detecting defects.
- Adaptability. The software must be adaptable for different companies' applications. This would be a true competitive advantage over existing inspection software.

The software that needs to be developed for your inspection system includes:

- Software that drives motors to move to different locations of the circuit board.
- Software that generates an image of the circuit board in the computer.
- Software that analyzes the image to detect defects.

Your other responsibilities include:

- Identifying and procuring hardware on which the software will run.
- Identifying and procuring existing commercial software packages that can be used to implement the system.

In your previous job, you successfully developed software to run on a different type of inspection system. You understand the many technical challenges of developing an automated inspection system. Since you've developed a similar product before, you have strong feelings about how the software should be developed. As a manager, you must be able to share your technical expertise with your team members and manage their development as well as the development of the software. You will walk a tightrope balancing the following factors:

- Meeting time constraints.
- Developing a quality product.
- Keeping team members productive by understanding what they are capable of accomplishing.
- Keeping team members motivated by understanding their needs.

DECISION 1: DECIDING WHO TO HIRE

Two years ago, when you first started the company, Gary, the vice president of Circuit Scan, approached you and related a discussion he had with Bob, the president of Circuit Scan. "Bob and I will be making a presentation to potential investors in one month. We need to develop an outline of what type of people we need to develop the software, how many people we need, and how long it will take to develop software for the Computers Unlimited machine."

"I'll give it my best shot, but there are still a number of unknowns to determine," you respond, feeling both excited and uneasy. You've never had to plan anything so big and with so much at stake!!

"Just put down what you know and come talk to me if you get stuck or want more advice!" comforts Gary.

Here it is, your first opportunity to mold your company and influence its future. By developing this plan, you will determine general guidelines for how the software is to be developed, who you need to help you develop it, and how long it will take. The software development plan will outline who your team members will be and what you'll be delegating to them. This is the opportunity to pinpoint the expertise and skills you need for the development of the product. You put the types of software that need to be developed into three categories:

Most difficult.   Software that analyzes images for defects. This complex task requires someone with experience and creativity.

Moderately difficult.   Software tools that aid the development of the software to analyze the images (for example, tools to store images in the computer, tools to make simple calculations on an image, etc.). You need someone with a fair amount of experience to determine what tools are useful.

Least difficult.   Software to manipulate the motors. This pretty straightforward, well-defined task involves developing a user-friendly interface to existing software.

You consider various staffing alternatives. You could hire all inexperienced professionals. This approach has the advantage that inexperienced team members will be receptive to learning, and you can instill your likes, dislikes, and knowledge. The disadvantage of this approach is that it will require a lot of your time for on-the-job training. You will be the only expert, and you will be less likely to get feedback on your ideas and strategies. You will probably have to do some of the software development yourself. Salaries will be lower, but the process will probably take longer and require a lot of your time. You will grant low levels of authority and give your staff small, specific tasks to implement. You will coordinate the overall picture.

You could hire all experienced professionals, a costly alternative in terms of salaries. Experienced professionals will require less of your time for training and management, but you risk having less control over the final outcome. These people won't want you to tell them how to do their jobs. They'll want to know what they are supposed to be doing but not how they're supposed to do it. If you tell them how to do their jobs, they'll probably lose motivation. These people will give you feedback and won't always agree with your ideas. If you get a good, compatible group of experienced people, you will develop a quality product in record time. If you get an incompatible group of experienced people, you will have to manage a larger number of people problems.

A third approach is to hire a mix of both experienced and inexperienced personnel. You can hire one or two experienced people to help develop the difficult software and use inexperienced people to develop the less demanding software. You can probably leave the experienced people alone once they know the responsibilities of their task and spend time training the less experienced people. You will rely on the experienced people to achieve their level of technical capabilities with low levels of interaction (e.g., Level D authority). The others will require Levels A, B, or C authority. With this approach you will probably be doing a fair amount of technical work to help the inexperienced professionals develop their skills.

Alternatives

Which of the following strategies will you use for hiring your software development team?

1. Hire all experienced professionals who have quite a few years of experience in the particular areas you need.

2. Hire all inexperienced software personnel that you will train and teach.

3. Hire approximately equal numbers of experienced and inexperienced personnel.
4. Hire a greater number of inexperienced software developers than experienced software developers.
5. Hire a greater number of experienced than inexperienced software developers.

WHAT IS YOUR CHOICE?   _____

Recommended Solution

5. HIRE A GREATER NUMBER OF EXPERIENCED SOFTWARE DEVELOPERS THAN INEXPERIENCED PERSONNEL.

Rationale

1. Approach 1 might not be the best approach for you as a new manager. You still have strong views about how things are to be done technically, and, as a manager, you need to learn to let team members take over these responsibilities. The combination of a new manager with all experienced professionals will lead to frustration on everyone's part.

2. If you choose approach 2, you are committing a low level of delegation. You are taking very few risks because you will be maintaining most of the control for the product. You will probably be working long hours. As time pressure increases, you may lose patience in training your new team members. You will not be delegating enough work.

3, 4. Approaches 3 and 4 are both viable alternatives. These approaches will teach you how to give up some control and new team members how to gradually assume new responsibilities.

5. Approach 5 is probably the best for a small start-up company like Circuit Scan. This approach will bring on a large number of highly qualified professionals who can act as equals in determining design strategies. This strategy will only require training time for a small number of new professionals. This approach will stretch a new manager's management capabilities. You can delegate low levels of authority to the new professionals, but high levels of authority to the experienced professionals.

DECISION 2: ALLOCATING WORK TO YOUR TEAM MEMBERS

For the purposes of setting a scenario, let's say you end up with a mix of experienced and inexperienced personnel. You prefer to have mostly inexperienced people on your staff, but after interviewing, you ended up hiring three experienced personnel and one new college graduate.

You originally wanted more inexperienced than experienced personnel because you felt it was a cost-effective alternative and you're not yet comfortable in the management role. You feel a need to maintain a high level of control over the technical development of the product. You are confident that you know what it takes to get a good product out the door, and you want to maintain the proper controls to ensure that your technical judgment is used throughout the development of the product. You feel that having a staff of mostly inexperienced personnel would have made it easier for you to maintain control. You wanted one or two experienced personnel to take responsibility for the difficult software. As it works out, it was hard finding people with the right qualifications. However, you are excited about the team. You believe they are a good group of intelligent people who are dedicated to quality. Three of the four have a proven track record. Following is a description of the qualifications of each of the people you hired.

Mark

- Bachelor's degree in physics.
- 12 years software development experience.
- For the last two years Mark has been an independent consultant for a variety of area companies.
- Looking forward to becoming part of a more stable environment.
- Enjoys technical work. Has had good software experience in areas required by your most difficult software tasks.

Tom

- M.S. computer science, B.S. mathematics.
- 15 years software development experience especially with computer graphics.
- Successfully led some small projects.
- Was recruited away from a competitor with a reputation for burning out employees. Most don't last more than two years. Tom managed to last six, an indication of his stamina and commitment.
- More interested in technical work than management.

Nancy

- M.S. computer science, B.A. mathematics
- Eight years of a variety of software development experience, particularly in the area of artificial intelligence.
- Strong, general-purpose software development skills in a variety of areas.
- Led a variety of small projects (2 to 4 people each).

Dave

- New college graduate with degrees in engineering and computer science.
- Good academic credentials.
- Good personality.
- Alert and perceptive in the interview.

Everyone you hired seems to be intelligent, easy-to-get-along-with, and eager to take the new job. Now that you have the team put together, you need to decide how to divide the work. To get a feel for how to do this, you find a reference in a software planning guide for a list of tasks that software managers are responsible for. You go through the list and

- Determine which items on the list are not relevant for your project,
- Which items on the list you should do yourself, and
- Which items on the list you can delegate to Mark, Tom, Dave, or Nancy.

Alternatives

Please check the appropriate columns indicating the guidelines you will use for delegating tasks. The "Don't Do It" column means you believe the task is not relevant for your project. The "Assign It" column indicates that you will have Mark, Tom, Dave, and/or Nancy take responsibility. You may still need to help them with the task, but they will do most of the work. The "You Do It" column indicates the task is one you should do yourself. Remember, these are just *general* guidelines.

	Don't Do It	Assign It	You Do It
1A. Budgeting/scheduling: determining how much money to allocate and planning goals and deadlines			
1B. Schedule/budget monitoring			
2A. Administrative tasks: memos, miscellaneous requests from your boss, miscellaneous reports, etc.			
2B. Reports to your direct managers			
2C. Reports to the board of directors			
2D. Reports to the customer			
3A. Materials/purchasing			
3B. Capital purchasing			
4. Customer interface: determining customer requirements, answering customers' questions, giving customer demonstrations			
5A. Unanticipated technical problems			
5B. Unanticipated personal problems			
5C. Unanticipated business problems			
6A. Technical development of product			
6B. Documentation of product			
6C. Quality assurance of product			

Recommended Solutions

	Don't Do It	Assign It	You Do It
1A. Budgeting/scheduling		X	
1B. Schedule/budget monitoring			X
2A. Administrative tasks		X	
2B. Reports to your direct managers			X
2C. Reports to the board of directors			X
2D. Reports to the customer		X	
3A. Materials/purchasing		X	
3B. Capital purchasing		X	
4. Customer interface		X	X
5A. Unanticipated technical problems		X	
5B. Unanticipated personal problems			X
5C. Unanticipated business problems		X	X
6A. Technical development of product		X	
6B. Documentation of product		X	
6C. Quality assurance of product		X	

Rationale

1. Budgets/scheduling. Schedules and budgets are an important part of developing a product. Schedules and budgets set baselines and establish goals. It's good to involve team members in the determination of schedules and budgets, but it's your responsibility to monitor schedules and budgets. Budgets and schedules are mechanisms for measuring and monitoring performance. They set standards for the team members. Team members feel ownership and involvement if they're allowed to participate in determining schedules. Inexperienced team members like Dave might not be involved in scheduling at first. But as they become more competent at their jobs, they should take on more scheduling responsibilities. More experienced people should be involved in the scheduling process.

2. Administrative tasks. Delegate as many administrative tasks as possible. A task that might be routine and boring to you can be challenging and provide avenues of growth for team members.

3. Materials and capital purchasing. You should oversee the purchasing of materials and capital as it relates to monitoring the budget, but you should not be too involved in the actual process. You might have to be involved initially until your team members understand the business better and you gain trust in their judgment. Eventually have your team members performing these tasks.

4. Customer interface. Interfacing with customers is important for both you and your team members. Some managers like to do the initial customer interface (that is, meeting the customer) and then have their team members take over. Use judgment on this one, but try to delegate when appropriate.

5. Unanticipated technical, personal, and business problems. Let your team members handle the technical problems. You should handle personal problems. Try to let your team members handle as many business problems as feasible.

6. Technical development, documentation, and quality assurance of product. This is probably one of the hardest things for a new manager to delegate, but let your team members have this responsibility—and let them become the experts!! If you are truly committed to becoming an effective manager—let go!!

DECISION 3: DELEGATING A TASK

You have your staff, and you've determined general guidelines as to what you are and aren't going to delegate. Now it's time to actually delegate. For the purposes of the scenario, you will be deciding how to delegate a task to Mark. You want Mark to develop the software that analyzes images of circuit boards to determine if there are any defects. You need to decide how much authority you will grant Mark.

Relevant characteristics about Mark's experience include:

- Strong technical background.
- Relevant technical experience.
- As an independent consultant, Mark was responsible for hustling business, defining and implementing projects, and guaranteeing customer satisfaction.

Computers Unlimited prepared a list of defects they want to be able to detect and the level of accuracy and throughput they need to achieve. You give the information to Mark and communicate explicitly what he needs to accomplish:

- The types of defects his software must be able to detect.
- The percentage of each of the defects his software must be able to detect.
- The speed at which his software must run.

Now you need to decide what level of authority to give Mark to accomplish this task. The following sections summarize various authority levels; see Chapter 4 for a more complete explanation.

Level A, no authority. If the assignment is especially important or difficult, if the team member is new, or if the type of assignment is new to him or her, it's often wise for you to assume all authority.

This level of authority should be used as infrequently as possible, however, since it indicates a low level of trust.

Even so, use this level when you have doubts about the successful completion of a task or when the task is so important that you want a high degree of involvement.

Level B, minimal authority. As the team member gains experience, it's desirable to allow him greater latitude in action.

This method allows the team member to have a say in the determination of his goals and performance standards, keeps you informed of the team member's progress, and gives you an opportunity to intervene if difficult problems arise.

Level C, medium authority. This level of authority allows the team member to make some levels of decisions without you.

For this level of authority, the team member sets the goals, plans, and performance standards. The team member then acts autonomously (with regular status reports to you) and consults you only if he encounters a particularly difficult problem or customer.

Level D, complete authority. When the team member has become a trusted employee who has demonstrated competence in completing the type of task assigned, you can grant complete authority. You will be completely removed from the assignment, even after it's completed. This is the level managers should hope to achieve with most team members on most assignments. When properly executed, this level gives you more discretionary time and the confidence that all work is being completed as scheduled.

With this level of authority, you have only minimal interaction with the team member in the form of a regular status report.

Alternatives

What level of authority will you delegate to Mark?

1. Level A, no authority
2. Level B, minimal authority
3. Level C, medium authority
4. Level D, complete authority

YOUR CHOICE: _____

Recommended Solution

3. DELEGATE A MEDIUM LEVEL OF AUTHORITY TO MARK.

Rationale

Mark is too experienced for Level A authority (no authority at all). He owned his own consulting company where he was responsible for getting new clients and keeping them satisfied. Mark had to be able to set his own goals and performance standards. Mark also has a lot of relevant technical experience, and he should be competent at handling most of the technical problems that come up.

Mark might not mind assuming lesser levels of authority, but as a manager you should be spending your time managing and not doing jobs that can be performed by your team members. And Mark will be more motivated if you grant him more authority for the project!

The highest level of authority is probably too much considering you are a new manager and Mark is a new employee. You need a minimum amount of communication and interaction in order to establish your relationship and mutual trust. Mark needs to know what you expect of him, and you need to determine what he is capable of handling.

With a medium level of authority, Mark will outline the goals and performance standards for the project. You will review and give your acceptance/disapproval of the goals and performance standards that Mark sets up. Make sure that the performance standards outline what you both understand to be superior, average, and poor performance!

DECISION 4: MONITORING THE DELEGATION

You delegate the recommended level of authority to Mark (Level C, medium authority). Mark is eager to start on the project and impress you with his work. Mark returns the next day with a set of goals, a schedule, and a description of the performance standards for the task. You zero in on the schedule and performance standards:

Schedule

The customer wants a beta site in one year. Mark sets the following deadlines for the previous set of tasks:

1. Document the types and characteristics of the defects to be detected.
2. Review the defects document with the key personnel at Computers Unlimited.
3. Develop the requirements for identifying these defects in an image of a circuit board.
4. Review these requirements with other members of Circuit Scan.
5. Design algorithms to detect the defects.
6. Implement algorithms to detect the defects.
7. Test the algorithms on boards provided by the customer for accuracy and speed.
8. Develop a set of documentation for the software developed.

Performance Standards

The performance standards Mark sets are:

Superior performance: Beating the one-year deadline, beating the throughput and accuracy requirements.

Good performance: Meeting the one-year deadline, throughput and accuracy requirements.

Poor performance: Missing any one of the above.

You look these over and decide that Mark did a good job. You agree with what he proposes. Once you agree on the responsibilities, goals, and performance standards of the project, you need to determine a way to monitor Mark's progress. How and how much will you be monitoring the task?

Alternatives

How will you monitor Mark's performance? Choose one or more of the following items, and rank them in priority order.

1. Frequently stop by Mark's desk for an informal discussion.
2. Ask Mark to submit written status reports to you.
3. Get feedback from other people (customers, coworkers) on Mark's progress.
4. Leave Mark alone until he tells you the job is done. Mark is competent and experienced to handle it on his own.

Recommended Solution

1, 3, and 2.

Rationale

The riskiest thing you could do would be to leave Mark alone and count on him to meet the goals and standards. You are not familiar with Mark's abilities yet, and he is not familiar with you. Install the proper controls in the delegation to make sure the goals and standards are met. The first three choices are all effective means of monitoring performance. Each mechanism gives you slightly different information about the performance.

1. Stop by Mark's desk and have an informal discussion with him—especially at first, before you are familiar with his abilities and style. This lets Mark feel that you are concerned with his progress. Don't be nosy, be open. Ask him how the project is going—and what frustrations he is encountering. This will help you learn more about Mark's personality and work style.

3. Get feedback from other people (customers, coworkers) on Mark's progress. You can learn a lot about Mark from other people who work with him!

2. Ask Mark to submit written status reports to you. Written status reports are good for documenting and tracking progress. However, relying purely on written status reports does not introduce the human element, which is probably necessary for your situation. Another problem with written status reports is they usually contain only positive information—not problems.

DECISION 5: EVALUATING THE DELEGATION

Let's say you decide to leave Mark alone assuming he is competent to complete the task on his own. To your dismay, Mark informs you that he isn't going to make the deadline. Mark finishes the project one month late. How are you going to handle this?

Alternatives

Choose one of the following methods for handling Mark's performance.

1. Let it go, chalk it up to experience.
2. Meet with Mark and discuss what went wrong.
3. Let it go for now, but mention the delay in Mark's next performance appraisal.

YOUR CHOICE: _____

Recommended Solution

2. MEET WITH MARK AND DISCUSS WHAT WENT WRONG.

Rationale

The worst thing you can do for both yourself and Mark is to let the situation go by unmentioned. If this happens, you probably won't trust Mark in the future. The second worst way to handle it is to not mention anything to Mark until his next performance appraisal. Mark needs to be held accountable for his actions. Mark needs feedback on his performance, and you need feedback on your delegation style. Both of you need to determine a more effective method for delegating in the future!

ENDNOTES

1. Thomas R. Horton, "Delegation and Teambuilding: No Solo Acts Please," *Management Review,* September 1992, p. 59.
2. Peter Burrows, "Power to the Workers," *Electronics Business,* October 7, 1991, p. 98.

Chapter 1

1. Everett T. Suters, "Overdoing It," *INC.,* November 1986, pp. 115–16.
2. Thomas R. Horton, "Delegation and Teambuilding: No Solo Acts Please," *Management Review,* September 1992, p. 60.
3. Donald W. Huffmire, "Learning to Share the Load," *Nation's Business,* September 1987, pp. 30, 32.
4. Thomas A. Stewart, "New Ways to Exercise Power," *Fortune,* November 6, 1989, p. 64.
5. Lawrence L. Steinmetz, *The Art and Skill of Delegation* (Boston: Addison-Wesley, 1976), p. 10.

Chapter 2

1. David K. Lindo, "Delegating Decisions," *The Executive Female,* January/February 1986, pp. 19–21.
2. Linda Swindal, "Delegate, Delegate!" *Working Woman,* July 1985, pp. 18, 23.
3. Joshua Hayatt, "No Way Out," *INC.,* November 1991, pp. 78, 90.
4. James M. Jenks and John M. Kelly, *Don't Do. Delegate!* (New York: Franklin Watts, 1985), p. 116.

5. Timothy W. Firnstahl, "Letting Go," *Harvard Business Review*, September-October 1986, pp. 15–16.
6. As reported in "Delegation: A Tool That Increases Management Efficiency—Part 2," *Small Business Report*, July 1986, pp. 42–43, 71–75.
7. Charles D. Pringle, "Seven Reasons Why Managers Don't Delegate," *Management Solutions*, November 1986, pp. 26–30.
8. Jenks and Kelly, *Don't Do. Delegate!* p. 133.

Chapter 3

1. James M. Jenks and John M. Kelly, *Don't Do. Delegate!* (New York: Franklin Watts, 1985), pp. 143–47.
2. Thomas R. Horton, "Delegation and Teambuilding: No Solo Acts Please," *Management Review*, September 1992, p. 61.
3. I. Thomas Sheppard, "The Art of Delegating," *Management World*, March 1984, pp. 26–29.
4. "Delegation: The Strongest Productivity Tool Management Can Utilize—Part I," *Small Business Report*, June 1986, pp. 38–43.

Chapter 4

1. Paul Hersey and Ken Blanchard, *Management of Organizational Behavior: Utilizing Human Resources*, 6th ed. (Englewood Cliffs, NJ: Prentice-Hall, 1993), pp. 416–17.
2. Ibid., pp. 421.
3. Ibid., p. 416.
4. Ibid., p. 439–40.
5. Dale D. McConkey, *No-Nonsense Delegation* (New York: AMACOM, 1974), pp. 138–41.
6. Hersey and Blanchard, *Management of Organizational Behavior*, p. 448.

Chapter 5

1. Paul Hersey and Kenneth Blanchard, *Management of Organizational Behavior: Utilizing Human Resources,* 6th ed. (Englewood Cliffs, NJ: Prentice-Hall, 1993), p. 435.
2. Thomas A. Stewart, "New Ways to Exercise Power," *Fortune,* November 6, 1989, p. 58.
3. Ibid., pp. 438–49.

Chapter 6

1. Peter Burrows, "Power to the Workers," *Electronics Business,* October 7, 1991, p. 100.

Chapter 7

1. Timothy W. Firnstahl, "Letting Go," *Harvard Business Review,* September-October 1986, p. 14.

Index

A

Accountability, 12–13
  without authority, 67
  in evaluation, 101–2
  failure of, 112
  of team members, 102–4
Accurate measurement, 82–83
Activity reports, 87
Adequate frequence, 83–84
Agreement, 101
Art and Skill of Delegation
  (Steinmetz), 11
Assignment log, 84–85
Attainable goals, 59
Authority, 11–12
  case study, 131–34
  diminished, 21–22
  failure to delegate, 108
  levels of, 66–71
  mistakes in granting, 67–68
  personal, 68
  rescinding, 93–94
  undercutting, 110
Aversion to risk, 22–23

B

Behavior reinforcement, 102
Biased controls, 92
Blanchard, Ken, 58, 78, 88, 139,
  140
Bossiness, 23
Burrows, Peter, 138, 140

C

Case study, 117–37
Coaching, 89–90
Commensurate authority, 67
Commitment, 73–74
Communication
  clear, 101
  of context and relevance,
    60–63
  effective, 55–57
  establishing rewards, 74–75
  lack of adequate explanation,
    108–9
  of obligation and commitment,
    73–74
  open, 82
  of performance standards,
    63–66
  of responsibilities, 57–59
  of support levels, 72–73
Competitiveness, 105
Complex situations, 49
Confidence, lack of, 22–24
Confidential tasks, 49
Constructive criticism, 99
Context, 60–63
Controls, 78–79
  biased, 92
  effective system of, 81–84
  internally consistent, 84
  statistical, 88
  system problems, 91–93
  tight versus loose, 79–81

Other excellent resources available from Irwin Professional Publishing . . .

THE CORPORATE COMMUNICATOR'S QUICK REFERENCE

Peter Lichtgarn

(192 pages)
This essential guide explains the duties, responsibilities, and functions of today's corporate communicator by anticipating the challenges and answering the questions communicators face daily.
ISBN: 1–55623–892–4

LEADING TEAMS

Mastering the New Role

John H. Zenger, Ed Musselwhite, Kathleen Hurson, and Craig Perrin

(275 pages)
Focuses specifically on the role of the leader as the key to long-term success. This book shows how managers can carve an enduring and vital position for themselves in a team environment.
ISBN: 1–55623–894–0

SURVIVE INFORMATION OVERLOAD

The 7 Best Ways to Manage Your Workload by Seeing the Big Picture

Kathryn Alesandrini

(225 pages)
You'll discover how to use innovative techniques so you can manage information efficiently, prevent paper buildup, make meetings more effective, capture ideas, and organize thoughts for enhanced productivity.
ISBN: 1–55623–721–9

Available at fine bookstores and libraries everywhere.

1. How did you find out about this Briefcase Book?

☐ Bookstore ☐ Irwin Catalog
☐ Advertisement ☐ Convention
☐ Flyer ☐ Other Catalog
☐ Sales Rep
other _____

2. Was this book provided by your organization or did you purchase this book for yourself?

☐ individual purchase
☐ organizational purchase

3. Are you using this book as a part of a training program?

☐ yes ☐ no

4. Did this book meet your expectations?

☐ yes ☐ no

(please explain) _____

_____

_____

_____

5. What other topics would you like to see addressed in this series?

(Please list)

_____

_____

_____

6. ☐ Please have a sales representative call me.

I am interested in:
☐ bulk purchase discounts
☐ custom publishing

7. ☐ Please send me a catalog of your products.

_____
Name

_____
Title

_____
Organization

_____
Address

_____
City, State, Zip

_____
Phone

BUSINESS REPLY MAIL

FIRST CLASS   PERMIT NO. 99   HOMEWOOD, IL

POSTAGE WILL BE PAID BY ADDRESSEE

IRWIN
Professional Publishing
Attn: Cindy Zigmund
1333 Burr Ridge Parkway
Burr Ridge, IL 60521-0081